The Nature of Mind Realities

SUE MAISANO, PHD

This book is dedicated to those who are awakening to the power of their own mind.

Contents

About Sue Maisano 7

Message from Sue Maisano...9

Matter is no "Matter" 11

"Matter" is the Product of Consciousness 15

Why Matter Feels so Real?..20

How Life Events Happen 24

Mind Pathway: From Energies "Outside" to Perceptions
by The Mind..29

The Mind Within the Framework of the Body – Sensing............34

The Mind Within the Framework of the Body – Reacting 37

Four Stages of Mental Processing...41

Conscious, Subconscious, and the Soul Mind 51

The Conscious Mind Does Not Exist..54

The Illusionary False Self – The Ego...58

Your True Self - Soul Being...62

The Illusion of Time – Clock Time is Not "Time" 67

The Illusion of Time – "Past" and "Future" Are Not "Time" 69

"Time" is Constant Change: Now is All You Have 72

The Illusion of Time: Change Your "Past" or "Future" to
Benefit Your NOW 76

The Illusion of Time: How to Benefit Yourself in
Conscious Creation 80

Conscious Creation, Letting Go of Reasoning and Logic 85

Beliefs: The Boundaries Within Which You Create Your
Personal Reality...92

Peace and Harmony: What You Truly Want 97

Mind Reality is The Only Reality There is – And You Are
an Expression of Higher Consciousness.....................................100

About Sue Maisano

Sue Maisano is a Chinese American healer, spiritual life coach and mindset coach.

Sue came to the United States at the age of 23 to pursue PhD studies in neurobiology at Wesleyan University in Middletown, Connecticut.

Her memoir *The Healing Journey: How a Poor Chinese Village Girl Became an American Healer* (https://mindrealities.com/the-healing-journey) documented her journey of how she overcame serious life challenges including her mom's strange illness and subsequent suicidal attempt, her family poverty, how fate manifested her unlikely chance of coming to America for higher education, her marriage to a loving Irish-Italian husband, her spiritual awakening, and answering her calling to healing and personal empowerment work.

Sue Maisano embodies Eastern and Western wisdom, bridges science and spirituality. She lives in Southington, Connecticut with her loving husband and 3 beautiful children.

Visit https://MindRealities.com for Sue's services.

Message from Sue Maisano

Soon after he received his Nobel Prize in Physics in 1918, Max Planck said, "We have now discovered that there is no such thing as matter; it is just all different rates of vibration designed by an unseen intelligence".

A pioneer physicist who studied matter under scientific scrutiny all his life reached the conclusion of matter being energy. We as laymen cannot blind ourselves anymore.

Everything is vibrational energy.

The world we see, hear, touch, smell and feel are a pool of vibrations, energy that is pulsing, all-encompassing, permeating everything.

Objects, liquid, gases, the earth, the moon, the sun, the stars, plants, rocks, oceans, air, human body, thoughts, emotions, event happenings are nothing but vibrational energies.

The understanding and utilization of the energy nature of everything is very important to us, because it is through workings with the law of energies that we can achieve what we want, be it healing, improving relationships or obtaining wealth.

It is imperative to awaken to the true nature of reality because it impacts every single aspect of us.

I attempt to explain the nature of mind reality in layman language in this book so everyone, regardless of education, regardless of religion, regardless of prior beliefs can grasp it with clarity and start using the laws of the Universe to achieve their goals, no matter how far-reaching it seems at the moment.

Through reading this book and understanding the concepts within you will also be able to achieve peace with life's situations and begin to make positive changes in accordance with the laws of the Universe.

I will begin the book with everyday knowledge that we already know but are not aware that we know, or perhaps always take it for granted. This is to open up our mind to explore bigger questions.

Then together we will dive deeper, through the lens of scientific studies, into the building blocks of matter and understand why solid matter is energy and how it appears "solid".

Next, we will explore the workings of our mind.

Then together we will look at the illusion of time and how to use it properly.

The reason that physical reality is the way it appears is because of our conscious participation in creating the reality. By our own behavior of observation of reality, we create it the way it is.

Our mind creates the reality that we see, hear, touch, smell and feel. Our mind also holds the key to higher consciousness where our true nature of being resides. Therefore, it is by tuning into our deeper minds that we can pill off the illusions and perceive the true nature of reality.

We can create with intention; we manifest energies into solid things and event happenings. We are creators because of the power of our mind.

Our mind truly is our greatest gift.

"The mind is the greatest power in all of creation." said J.B. Rhine, the founder of parapsychology, and I couldn't agree with him more.

"If you want to find the secrets of the universe, think in terms of energy, frequency and vibration." — Nikola Tesla.

Great minds in history understood the essence of the Universe is vibrational energy.

Now in layman language regardless of background, everyone can understand this profound wisdom. And in understanding the true essence of the Universe you unleash your greatest power within you.

Now let's begin our exciting journey.

Matter is no "Matter"

Did you know that, whenever you watch a movie, whatever you see on the screen is nothing but projections of static images?

How come static images make you feel the continuous motion that makes sense?

These static images are presented to you in super-fast speed beyond the mind's perception of the "gap" between the images. Therefore, you observe continuous motion rather than individual static pictures.

Movies are motion pictures. It works because of the illusion of the mind.

Static images flashing rapidly beyond the mind's perception of a "gap" provides the experience of continuous motions where stories deploy, which then moves you on the mental and emotional plane.

Cartoons work the same way.

The cartoon artist draws picture after picture and compiles them into a sequence.

This may be a scene of a person running, with a series of pictures, first with the person starting to lift a leg and then in the next picture the leg lifting a little higher, while everything else remains relatively the same as the first picture. The next one has the leg a little higher, then the next. Then the picture will show the leg starts to drop, and so on until there is a step forward.

After the series of pictures is completed, the artist can flip through the pictures at high speed so that it appears as continuous motion.

Again, the mind fills in the "gap" and perceives the continuity from which the story can take shape. It is nothing but an illusion of the mind put to good use.

This is common knowledge that we all know of.

Similarly, physical reality and the material world works the same way; it is an illusion of the mind. It is a different "gap" we are filling in.

We believe that matter is "solid", that it is out "there". However, this is simply an illusion of the mind similar to the process of how we make static images into continuous motion. Matter is, in essence, energy that the mind perceives as "solid".

When scientists go down deeper and deeper into matter, dividing and dissecting it into its smallest elements, they found the fundamental thing that comprises every physical element. They called it atoms, which means 'indivisible' in Greek.

There are around 120 types of atoms, and they combine in different patterns to form molecules and, ultimately, what we see as matter in the Universe.

Logic tells that atom is also matter because it is the building blocks of matter. Dividing matter to its smallest elements should not change its nature of being matter, right?

You would certainly expect when a skyscraper is broken down into its smallest elements you get each individual brick, which is also solid just like the building itself.

By the same token, atoms were expected to be "matter", meaning things that exist on our physical plane.

Surprisingly, this is not the case.

At close scientific examination, an atom contains a positively charged core particle called a nucleus in the middle and negatively charged particles, called electrons, circling around it.

The positive charge of the nucleus and negative charges of all electrons are of equal strength and therefore cancel each other out. Therefore, atom has no electrical charge overall.

The nucleus accounts for over 99.9 percent of the mass of the atom, yet the space it takes up is less than 1/10,000th of its total volume. The sizes of electrons are also extremely small within the atom.

This means that the weight, the actual "stuff" of the atom takes up almost no space. The sizes of the nucleus and electrons are **negligible** compared to the space they seem to "fill".

Put simply, atom is composed of mostly empty space!

Since atoms are the building blocks of matter, this did not seem to make sense at first glance. It means that matter is practically empty space!

If you were to condense the entire galaxy and eliminate the empty space within the atoms, everything within the physical world would fit into the parking lot of a football stadium.

A human body, when the empty space within matter is eliminated, would be smaller than the tip of a needle.

That shows how much "stuff" there is in matter. Literally, there is no "matter" in matter, it's primarily empty space.

It is as if when a skyscraper is broken down into its smallest elements, each individual brick, you found out that each individual brick is practically air, 99.9 percent empty space! There is simply no "stuff" to it.

Scientists' obsession with matter and the laws of physics that we knew of was shattered in the face of the discovery of the fundamental elements that compose matter. Matter is made of "empty space".

The physical world that we believed so solid and so real had nearly nothing in there. Imagine the shock and disbelief when the nature of atom was revealed with rigorous scientific studies.

It seems so counterintuitive to our perceptions of the physical world. How could it possible that the world we are in is mainly empty you ask? Yet it is a scientific truth based on observation. Not only you, scientists were baffled.

That's not the end of the story though. This seemingly empty space is not "empty", it is full of information, full of energy.

The behavior of the nucleus and electrons defies our understanding of the laws of classical physics, our well-accepted scientific principles tested for hundreds of years.

Atoms and smaller particles are called quantum particles, and the studies of them is termed quantum physics.

Quantum physics do not follow what we know as classical physics.

The electrons do not orbit around the nucleus as physical particles, instead they flash in and out of physical existence in a region surrounding the nucleus.

From the outside they look like a "cloud" around the nucleus, appearing in one place then disappear, then reappear in another spot, then disappear and reappear in yet another location. They are simply flashing in and out of our physical plane of existence.

Where an electron is found in a certain position along the orbit around the nucleus is a wave of probabilities; a matter of chance that fits mathematical calculations.

The weirdness doesn't stop there.

"Matter" is the Product of Consciousness

When *observed*, quantum particles stop behaving like "probability waves" and show features of a standard particle like a ping-pong ball would behave.

In other words, when being observed by consciousness, electrons behave like a standard particle in the physical plane. They were no longer flashing in and out of physical existence! They became something "solid" that's there upon our observation.

The simple act of *observing* changes the properties of quantum particles. Quantum particles have their own intelligence and it is impacted by our *consciousness.*

Whether quantum particles behave like probability waves or classic particles depends on whether or not we give them attention.

You can understand it this way, our simple act of observation pulls the quantum particles out of a higher dimension of energy plane.

For illustrations of how conscious observation of quantum particles changes them from probability waves to standard particle, search for "double slit experiment" on YouTube and you will see it in action.

Scientists speculate that matter does not exist when not being observed and comes into physical existence when being observed.

We behold them into the physical reality that we live in. That is to say, it is *us* who **created** the physical reality. We are "fixing" the physical world out of pools of energy pulsations.

Without our consciousness beholding matter, they would not appear "matter" at all; they are pure energy constantly flowing.

This may sound crazy to our everyday understandings, nonetheless it's an unbiased conclusion we had arrived to with rigorous scientific studies.

For example, the table in your living room does not exist until you or someone else observe it. It is in a state of vibrational energy flashing in and out of physical existence when not being observed by consciousness.

Conscious observation fix probabilities into solid particles. For things to manifestation into the physical there has to be conscious participation, otherwise it remains as invisible energies.

A philosophical thought experiment explored, "If a tree falls in a forest and no one is around to hear it, does it make a sound?"

The seeming existence of physical reality is co-created by conscious observation/perception by the mind. Without a mind, or some level of consciousness, observing it, it remains in a state of pure vibrational energies.

Consciousness manifest energies into physical plane. It is through our five senses that matter manifest and appear into the physical plane out of its energy nature. It is our conscious participation that makes matter the way it is.

There is no matter where there is no conscious participation.

Of course, there's also the question of what level of consciousness can become a creator?

Do cats and dogs count?

When they observe, do they create realities?

What about other animals?

What about plants and other forms of life?

What about rocks, water and other nature's element?

What is the minimum level of consciousness to create physical reality?

These questions are beyond the scope of this book, but I would like to provide some food for thought here for your own exploration.

Even though we are having a hard time in our everyday lives grasping and admitting that the nature of matter is intangible energies, science is now advanced enough to acknowledge it and use the discoveries from quantum physics.

You may not know that this seemingly weird phenomenon of quantum particles has already been applied to our daily lives: lasers, LED lights, and cell phones all use this technology.

Ever wondered why we can use cell phones and Wi-Fi even inside rooms with no windows and when the door is closed?

Electricity lights up our houses, runs electrical appliances and electronic devices, cooks our food, gives us heat, and more. Most of us could not imagine a life without electricity.

It can work because, in certain materials, such as metal, the negatively charged electrons within the atom are "loosely" attached to their nucleus and can flow in a circuit when driving by other types of energy such as magnetic force.

The use of electricity is based on the behaviors of quantum particles.

You will be amazed how the things we take for granted in our daily lives depend on the quantum structures of atom.

The point is this: the technology we take for granted is actually quite advanced and the science behind the quantum features of matter is being applied whether you know it or not.

How to reconcile classical physics that we are so familiar with and the seemingly weird new science discoveries called quantum physics?

How to make sense of everything including matter being energy?

How can we use the energy nature of reality to manifest a better life?

You will soon find out the answers.

It is not that we have to make an exception in classic physics to account for quantum physics. It is the other way around. The classical physical laws that we know are fundamentally a special case of quantum physics.

We are arriving at the higher truth through rigorous scientific research, which can then influence and therefore elevate the consciousness of the mass.

Quantum physics is *Universal*, and we are starting to recognize its significance and profound meaning.

This means that matter, for the most part, is empty space.

Matter is, in fact, waves of probabilities, and our understanding of physical reality must be rewritten.

What we know about physical reality might simply be a glimpse of the true reality behind the veil.

Luckily, you don't have to become a quantum physicist to understand the nature of matter.

In fact, quantum physicists are as shocked as you and I about their own discoveries and where it has taken them.

"If quantum mechanics hasn't profoundly shocked you, you haven't understood it yet." – Niels Bohr, Nobel Prize laureate in physics.

From a scientific perspective, we took a glimpse into the non-physical nature of matter and, therefore, were compelled to seek the ultimate truth and the nature of reality.

You don't have to be a scientist, having all the credentials. You don't have to conduct scientific studies to understand the true nature of realities, and in fact, as quantum physics already showed that our own conscious observation changes reality.

Therefore, any scientific studies are prejudiced in the first place because conscious observation and scrutiny is heavily involved.

I'm not disapproving science or anything, quite the contrary actually.

Science had brought us to the great understanding that we are at today. Science studies are objective and proof-driven; therefore, it is convincing.

However, I want you to understand that anyone can understand the true nature of reality, no scientific background needed.

Open up your mind and don't restrict your abilities to understand higher truth. Don't shy away from your exploration of consciousness and the nature of reality.

You are a conscious being, that's all you need for qualification.

We can no longer ignore the fact that there are higher realities than our physical one. Science had proved that the world we live in is energy.

David Bohm, one of the greatest quantum physicists said, thought creates the world then says, "I didn't".

Indeed, the physical world we are living in is created by our thought, by our conscious participation in physical reality. However, we may not be aware that we are the creator, we look outside of us and say, see the world is out there independent of me.

Now you are aware that you ARE the creator! You created your world with your consciousness.

Why Matter Feels so Real?

If the essence of matter is non-physical, why do we feel it is so "real" and so "solid"?

Why can you touch a table and sit on a chair?

Why can't you slip through a wall?

Isn't the world out there?

These are really important questions that only now we begin to recognize its significance. We had been so engrossed to and taking granted of physical realities that we weren't even curious about the most fundamental questions until now.

Matter feeling "solid" is an illusion of the mind, just as static images form the illusion of continuous motion in movies.

Since electrons travel so rapidly and appear to be a "cloud" around the nucleus in the form of waves of possibilities, matter "occupies" the vast space that the atom claims, giving us the illusion of "volume".

The mind cannot perceive the "empty space" within an atom because quantum particles are flashing so fast within this space, just as the mind cannot perceive the "gap" in movie pictures flashing past as a series of static images.

Essentially, matter is nothing but negative charges vibrating around positive charges at high speed, or you can say high "frequencies" or "vibrations". It keeps moving and vibrating, creating the illusion of filling up the space it seems to occupy.

In essence, matter is not matter as we know it; it is energy! This energy/frequency/vibration works with our conscious awareness to create the "physical" reality.

Our mind makes physical matter seem "real" but it's an illusion.

Quantum physics is *Universal*, however, on the scale that is big enough and visible to us, the classical physical laws that we know of for centuries apply perfectly, because "quantum features" shows themselves as such once on this grand scale.

The classical physics as we know it is a special case of quantum physics.

If you consider that your physical body is the real YOU, a view that you will find erroneous later in this book, then you are right in saying that you cannot slip through a wall.

But what if in essence you are a pure consciousness, pure energy?

What if the consciousness of the real you is not restricted by physical barriers?

Why can't you slip through a wall?

Physical reality ***does not exist***. It is an illusion of the mind and it moves us on the ***mental*** and ***emotional*** plane. There is no physical realty, only the perception of the mind. And the reason that it feels so real is because we operate our daily life through our physical bodies, with physically oriented sensory modalities that are tuned into the "system".

Let's go back to the movie example. Great movies allow you to suspend disbelief and forget your own "reality" temporarily. It moves you on the ***mental*** and ***emotional*** plane. In other words, what is changing in you while watching a movie is your ***energies***.

You might be so caught up in a movie that you identify with the main character or characters. You laugh or weep, depending on the scenario; you become part of the movie, totally immersed.

Coming out of the movie theater, you might be still thinking of the plot and it takes a little reorientation to readjust to your own everyday reality.

Unlike watching a movie, which have a very limited time frame, this movie that we are watching and living in called "physical reality" lasts a lifetime, and we are so caught up in it that we believe it is solid and real.

It does not mean that physical reality does not matter. A ball hitting the wall will bounce off it; it is the law of classical physics. Scientists studied for centuries on this grand level of physics and mechanisms apply perfectly as we already know.

But, no matter how real it seems to your senses, I draw your conscious mind to the possibility of higher realities. Perhaps you can open your mind to such an extent that you cultivate higher understanding and live with an expanded perspective?

As Einstein said:

> **Reality is merely an illusion, albeit a very persistent one.**

Great minds think alike. I will quote Nikola Tesla again:

> **If you want to find the secrets of the universe, think in terms of energy, frequency and vibration.**

David Bohm, one of the greatest quantum physicists said,

> **Thought creates the world then says, "I didn't".**

No matter how well-conceived this illusion of physical reality is, you have the option of living from a larger sense to get the most out of life by being the creator that you are.

Does this have anything to do with healing and empowerment? Absolutely!

The purpose of a deeper understanding of physical reality, and ultimately the nature of mind realities, is to heal and empower you so that you can live your life with a broader sense, where letting go of the physical trappings and the power of conscious creation becomes possible.

In short, true healing and empowerment requires that you understand the true nature of reality.

Many ailments and suffering in life are due to not being able to let go. Not being able to let go is a result of not seeing the higher truth of reality.

Over 2500 years ago Buddha had already perceived the "emptiness" in the physical world. Now our modern science is beginning to catch up with Eastern philosophies at the understanding level of the emptiness. However, mere intellectual understanding of the higher truth is only the beginning, to reach the feeling and being level is another journey.

How Life Events Happen

The implications of matter being energy is foundational.

Once this concept is fully understood and applied, you will step into your role of being a creator of physical reality, not only in influencing matter but in creating desirable life events.

You might have heard the phrase that we are the product of our environment. This is true with our old limited view of perception.

When you graduated from college, you are so thrilled that you partied like an animal.

When you get married, you feel loved as if you are on the clouds.

When you get your first job, you feel secure.

When you get your first raise, you feel powerful.

When you have your first baby, you are so proud.

When you are fired from your job, you are angry and upset. You fear that you won't be able to feed your family.

When you lose a family member, you are so heart broken.

When you have quarrels with your spouse, your in-laws, your parents, your children, or your friends, you feel so mad and pent up.

When you check on news or social media sites, you see politics upset you, or postings you hate, you feel drained, angry and frustrated.

When you drive on the road you see people not following the traffic rules and you feel disappointed and even rage.

You feel that you are the product of your own environment. If things outside of you are good, then you are happy. If things outside of you are bad, then you are miserable.

You simply react to your outer environment. You act as a victim with no control of how you feel. You are like a duckweed with no

24

attachment to anything and just simply flows anywhere with the water without self-control.

This is how the majority of people act in life. They respond/ react to their outer environment. They use the outer environment to feed their mind and let the outside to dictate how they feel inside of them. This is done unconsciously.

Things of the same nature/pattern keep happening to them because they are in this loop of using the outside to control their inside. What they get in life is quite predictable.

However, you will realize that this is placing the cart in front of the horse when you understand the nature of mind realities.

Consciousness co-creates matter by clasping probabilities into actual particles as we have discussed.

Likewise, future life events exist in the form of probabilities just as quantum particles.

At any given moment in life, you have countless potentials of future life events happening in your life.

Future potentials of good things happening and bad things happening co-exist. Which one is "fixed" into physical reality depends on your conscious participation, it depends on *how* you observe it, just as your consciousness manifest solid "matter" out of probabilities.

How are you observing your life events?

What is your attitude towards them?

What are you giving your attention to?

What you are giving attention to is what you are feeding energy to. You are "observing" your life events just as you are observing quantum particles.

By your conscious observation, you "fix" potentials into solid particles, in this case life events.

Therefore, from the pool of potentials you choose your future events by giving it thought.

Now, let's go back to how to switch your paradigm from letting outer environment control you to you determining your future life events.

What you need to do is to first realize your own power of conscious creation, your consciousness creates the physical world you are living in and the events in your life.

At any given moment in life, when you have negative feelings, ask yourself how you can change your attitude so you feel good.

Everything has duality.

When you feel bad, there must be a way you can feel good. The only danger is to be carried away by the bad feelings that you won't even consider the possibility of a good feeling. Don't be pulled into negative feelings unconsciously.

For example, if your dominant thought is fear that you won't be able to pay the next bill. When you have that feeling your focus is lack.

The opposite would be plenty. Make a decision to focus on plenty. It does not even have to be related to money. It could be anything, such as the bountiful mother nature. What you need to change is your feeling tone by choosing a new focus.

When you are bogged down by a negative feeling, what it tends to do is it breaks your wing of imagination and creativity. Your option of choices becomes very limited.

With our life driven by outer environment unconsciously, we would not choose to imagine a different scenario where a better future happens.

Let's use the feeling of lack of money as example again.

When you are stuck in that mode, you are not imagining money flowing to you. Your sole focus is lack, and therefore you are fixing your future potentials into more lack, which confirms the thing you feared – not being able to pay the bills.

When that happens it further confirms that your fear was legit, the new bad reality creates more feeling of lack and the loop continues on.

By default, most people use "what is" to determine "what will be", and let the environment drive their inner feelings. This is how they *observe* reality and fixing probabilities into realities. They focus on bad things happening in the form of fears or worries and pulling bad events out of infinite pools of pulsations of energies.

This type of reality creation is backwards and rigid and does not support your unlimited potential.

What is in your environment was manifested from your previous feelings and your previous choosing; the environment was the end result not the cause. Now if you use the environment to determine how you feel, then you will continue to progress on the same path.

To break the chain, you have to feel good internally, and imagination is a great tool.

Einstein said, "imagination is more important than knowledge."

Imagination is what can unleash your potential and live life in a much broader sense.

Imagination is unrestricted by current knowledge, current limitations, current outer environment. Imagination is what gives you wings and quantum leap.

Imagine a better future, imagine what would happen when your desired outcome occurs. Use your imagination to release you from the mental prison you have built.

How will you feel when your desire is manifesting?

Who will you be hanging out with?

What will you be doing to celebrate your success?

What would you see, hear, touch, smell and taste?

How would you feel vibrationally?

Make your desired outcome, which is not determined by your current situation, as vivid as you possibly can in your imagination. Fully live in your imagination with all your internal senses. Feel it as if it is happening right now. Don't entertain any doubt.

If you have to doubt, doubt your limitation.

When you do that, you are pulling your desired outcome towards you just as your consciousness fix probabilities into physical particles.

The Universe we live in is energy in nature and it is intelligent. Imagination is the fast dial to the higher vibration that holds our desired future. Imagination is happenings on a higher dimension beyond our physical plane. Imagination gets us closer to the source of creative energy.

Too many people were taught to ignore and suppress their imaginations since a young age that by the time they become adults they discredit imaginations, because imagination does not use the five physical senses and therefore deemed unreliable.

However, by understanding matter and future life events as probabilities fixing into the physical plane, you now realize that what your physical senses perceive are results, not the true essence or source.

On the other hand, your imagination carries you up to higher planes of reality closer to the source of where everything springs from.

How you observe your current life events, in other words your attitude, determines what future events will occur.

Your consciousness not only manifest matter into the physical plane, but also create life events out of potentials.

Mind Pathway: From Energies "Outside" to Perceptions by The Mind

W e never directly interact with our environment. The world around us is energy. The physical reality we are navigating within is energy pulsations manifested into the physical plane by our mind.

We are bathed in this infinite pool of energies and our five physical senses are our "filters" of different ranges of frequencies.

Our mind translates the frequencies of 430–770 THz into visible light. It also translates the frequencies of 20 to 20,000 Hz into audible sound.

For example, light waves shine upon on an object. The object then reflects the light wave, which reaches and activates the photoreceptors in our retina.

Then, an electrical magnetic signal is generated by the neurons involved, and it travels along our nervous system until it reaches the visual cortex, the headquarters within our brain that processes visual information.

In this pathway, our physical sense, sight, is the energy "filter". It channels the visible light wave energy, 430–770 THz, into an electromagnetic signal our brain can receive, and our mind can interpret as images.

Does the object we see really exist?

It appears on the physical plane as a solid object because of our conscious observation of it as we discussed earlier. In essence matter is a type of energy vibrations.

In terms of our physical sense of hearing, similar things happen. The sound waves are funneled into the ear canal and cause our eardrum to vibrate.

This vibrational signal is eventually transmitted into an electromagnetic signal by neurons and travels along the auditory nerve to reach the auditory cortex, the headquarters within our brain that processes auditory information.

In this pathway, our physical sense, hearing, is the energy "filter". It channels the energy frequency of 20 - 20,000 Hz through the auditory pathway for the brain to understand sound.

Each of our physical senses filter a particular range of frequencies of energies and translate them into electromagnetic signals within the body, which is also energy, to reach the corresponding brain centers. The brain then feeds the conscious mind where perception is formed.

It seems that we are living a physical life, but in reality, we never deal directly with a "physical" world "out there". We simply filter energies and create senses internally.

When signals arrive at the corresponding brain centers, they are still "raw"; they are simply electromagnetic signals. For example, in the process of seeing a beautiful flower versus seeing someone flip a middle finger, at the brain centers there is no "meaning" yet, you won't perceive an image of the flower or middle finger inside the structure of the brain. The brain contains the raw electromagnetic signals, or neuronal activities.

What happens next is that this raw electromagnetic signal is transferred to the mind.

The mind is not a physical structure like our brain, but is a form of intelligence on a higher plane, higher dimension beyond the physical plane that we live in.

How does this higher plane correlate with our physical body and space in general?

The mind occupies roughly the same space as our body.

Our Universe is energy in nature, and it operates on frequencies. Our true essence is energy, it is at our mind level, not brain, that things take on meaning.

Our mind is our gateway, our attunement to different levels of consciousness. Our conscious mind, the part that we are aware of, received input from the physical world through our sensory "filters", our five senses.

At our everyday frequency, we are attuned to the physical world and anchor our senses to the physical plane.

The matter that we perceive is a form of constant vibrating energy. Not only matter but other physical realities, such as sound and touch, are also vibrational energies. The only difference between them is "frequency".

Your senses are nothing but receptors of different "frequencies" of energies. For example, if the frequency falls in the range of 430-770 THz, it is perceived as visual. If the frequency is 20 Hz to 20k Hz, it is sound.

Our five senses (sight, hearing, taste, smell and touch) were created so that our sensory organs receive signals in different ranges of frequencies, which the marvelous mind transcribes into meaningful messages.

Each sensing faculty is so tuned into its own designated frequencies that typically you can't "hear" a color or "see" a sound. Yet they are synchronized in such a way that if you "see" an object, such as a stone, the touch sense of that stone will not feel liquidity; it's rock solid.

The sensing perceptions are "harmonious" when it comes to the interpretation of the physical reality. Your physical body is built perfectly to channel the physical world as the way it is, and it works with the mind to bring *sense* and *meaning* that we know of.

There is nothing but what is perceived by the mind. Most of the time, what we know as the conscious mind is tuned outwards to physical realities through our sensory organs. Physical realities are only real in the mind, which perceives through the vehicle of the body.

Do the ranges of frequencies that human beings sense covers the full range of frequencies out there?

Of course not.

The frequencies our five senses can perceive are only a small range of frequencies in the infinite pool of energies/frequencies/vibrations in the Universe.

There are many frequencies that escape our perception but can be picked up by animals.

For example, bats can hear what we term "ultrasound": when sounds bounce off objects and create an echo, bats can hear it and use this to locate objects. Their sensory organs are built to receive higher frequency sounds than humans and their minds work according to their sensory channeling, just as ours do.

Every species has its own "match" between the body (receiving frequencies) and mind (perceiving frequencies into meanings).

What we perceive with our sensory modalities is limited and it does not fully represent all there is, and every human being is distinctive too. There may be subtle differences in sensory perception and acuity from one person to the next.

Can we understand what the Universe is all about when all we trust is our *physical senses*?

Could there be more than what meets the eyes, ears and skin?

More importantly, should you seek a deeper understanding of reality to gain broader perspectives that enable you to navigate life better?

When we intentionally elevate our frequencies, we enter a higher reality where everything is different.

Our physical reality and this higher reality coexist in space and it takes changing our own frequencies/consciousness to experience the higher reality. There is not just one higher reality though, there are infinite realities at different frequency ranges, with realities higher than ours and those that are lower.

It's like the radio waves.

Different frequencies of radio waves coexist in the air surrounding us. The device we call radio can attune and dial into these frequencies.

If you dial into the frequency of 97.5 you hear messages clearly from this channel. When you change the frequency to 103.5, now you are listening to message from this new channel.

Do the frequencies of 97.5, 103.5, and other frequencies coexist in the air?

Of course they do!

But which channel signal you perceive is based on which frequencies you are tuned into. Your body is the radio.

From a wide range of frequencies, you attune into particular ones and only perceive messages from that chosen frequency, which by default is our five physical senses.

By filtering energies through our physical senses, we make sense of the physical world, while ignorant of a much larger world.

Our physical reality and higher/lower realities coexist in the space that we know of just like different radio frequencies coexist in air, which one you are perceiving is based on your attunement of frequencies. Your mind is the dial. By default we are channeled into what we know as physical reality.

As soul beings occupying a human body living a physical life, we are naturally attuned to the physical reality. We are anchored to this plane of existence.

Now, with this understanding, let's go back to the discussion of mind.

The mind is intelligence on a higher plane, and it occupies roughly the same space as the human body, with more concentrated energy around the brain area.

The Mind Within the Framework of the Body - Sensing

You see a beautiful flower right in front of you and you are **moved** by its beauty.

Does the image of the flower hit your eye, travel through your visual system and finally arrive in your mind?

Is that how you *see*?

No, that's not the case. There was never an image of a flower *until* your mind perceived it.

First, there must be light for you to see the flower or anything at all. The flower reflects light and, when the reflected light reaches your eye, it activates light-sensitive cells within the retina. The light sensitive cells, lots of them, then generate nerve impulses that travel through the pathway of the visual system reaching the brain.

The brain is the headquarters of neuronal signals, but it is not the "end station". The signal ultimately reaches your mind and is then deciphered into the image form that you *perceive*: a beautiful flower.

You did not see an *actual* flower; what you perceive and make sense of, in the form of the flower, is the *electromagnetic energy* reflected by the flower. Your mind translated everything for you and creates the meaning.

This "perceiving" part of your mind also receives internal information from other parts of the mind, such as permanent memories from the subconscious mind. You may feel happy that you have seen the flower, maybe even stunned by its perfection or moved to tears.

What happened exactly? Why do we react to things like this and perceive them as pleasant or unpleasant?

From an intellectual perspective, with our new understanding of the nature of the building blocks of matter, it is not hard to understand that the flower does not actually exist, since all physical reality is an illusion of the mind. But how did this illusion happen and how did the mind make sense of it?

Once the sensory information reaches us through the sensory organs, it is transmitted inside the body as *electromagnetic* signals, such as the visual information of the flower travelling to the brain.

These signals have no meaning *until* the brain sends the information to the mind to process it. The mind interprets and decodes the raw electromagnetic signal to "produce" the image or sound, or any other perceptions.

Any outside physical information must first be channeled through different sensory modalities of the body, then travel as raw electromagnetic signals to reach the brain, which then forwards the information to the mind, which is where things take on sense and meaning.

Essentially, the conscious mind perceives through the body through the sensory organs. Here I use the term "conscious mind", because the subconscious mind and "soul mind" may not require sensory organs in order to perceive.

To the conscious mind, the body reality is the only reality there is. The conscious mind draws the information from the brain, the brain from the sensory organs, and the sensory organs from the energies projected by the "physical" world.

So the flow of the signal is like this: Outside Energy – Sensory Organs – Within The Body – Brain – Conscious Mind. In this flow, the conscious mind does not directly interact with the outside world but simply deals with the body. It creates sensations that are faithful to what the body provides and does not go beyond the body's framework when using sensory modalities to perceive the world.

In fact, there is nothing "physical" in the pathway at all. Physical reality is what the mind gives meaning to; it exists ***in the mind,*** not outside. The mind never deals with the "raw" material from the so-called "physical reality". So, there is no reality other than what is perceived by the mind; in short, ***reality is in the mind***.

The conscious mind is confined by the framework of the body; it is in direct contact with the body. To perceive the outside world, your mind relies on the sensory organs.

The sensory organs are like antennas, filtering information to your mind. The conscious mind is like a transcriber; it can transcribe energies into perceptions of solid matter.

The Mind Within the Framework of the Body - Reacting

The mind not only perceives and generates sensations and feelings based on the information the body sends; it also sends out reactions as a response. What does the mind feedback to? Nothing but the body!

Imagine that you are in the woods, walking alone. You see a bear and you are so scared; your heartbeat increases, and your hands sweat. You end up screaming and you try to run away. Or perhaps you got so scared that your heartbeat went off chart and you died?

Had you not generated this series of dramatic reactions, the bear may have missed you, gone his own way, and you would have survived.

You see, it's all mental and reactions of the mind can only discharge onto the body. The reaction could be as obvious as activating the muscular system to run fast, as in the case with fight or flight response; or it could be as subtle as invisible changes in internal organs that only manifest into malfunctions over the course of time.

Unreleased emotions, attachments, desires, aversions, jealousies, hatred, and other emotions are all stored in the body parts. That's the only place this energy can go.

It may not be as quick and obvious as running away from a bear, but the body is still the only outlet for the mind to react to. The mechanism remains the same.

The mind never interacts directly with the "outside" world. It perceives what the body brings, and it reacts using the body.

To the everyday conscious mind, the body is the only reality there is; we have already seen that it does not operate outside the framework of the body. Likewise, to the body, mind reality is the only reality there is.

The body is a perfect mirror of the state of mind.

But here's the problem. To an uncultivated mind, these reactions can be quite harmful to the body. The uncultivated mind reacts to events, happenings, and people blindly, by default. When desirable events do not eventuate, the mind reacts with uncontrollable clinging and becomes miserable. When undesirable things happen, the mind generates aversion and also becomes miserable.

Human beings are often so attached to physical reality and dictated by outside happenings that they are ignorant of the illusion of their own mind. They don't realize that everything is mind creation, including their sufferings.

The uncultivated mind generates blind sensations and feelings according to what the body provides from a limiting perspective; the mind also reacts to these sensations and feelings blindly and generates adverse emotions, causing miserable feelings.

People then lose power and think that everything is outside of their control and that they are simply a victim of circumstances, situations, events, and other people.

Substance addiction is a good example. There's never an addiction to cigarettes, alcohol, or a particular drug. There's only addiction to the "sensations" and "feelings" generated by these substances. The sensations and feelings by substances are only temporary escapes from deeply buried emotions.

The mind reacts to the sensations, creates cravings, and won't settle until it finally experiences that desired sensation again. It is an example of the blind interaction between the mind and body, where the mind relies on outside triggers to make it feel a certain way or to cover up an undesirable feeling.

Unless one learns the truth of the mind, it reacts, reacts, and reacts endlessly, creating misery. There's nothing wrong with the sensation, every human being is bound to experience pleasant and unpleasant sensations, but blind mental reactions to a sensation can multiply it to the point of being unbearable.

Whatever situation you are in, no matter how painful it seems, is created by your own choice. Because you are so deep in the perceived "reality" that you confine yourself and close yourself off to other possibilities.

You may say "that's the way it is", it's "reality". But think about what reality really is. There's nothing outside of you but things that you perceive, interpret, and react to in your own mind. And you can change your mind like flipping a switch. So you can choose to become a master of your own mind rather than a victim. You can start to shift your reality whenever you so choose.

Since your mind is responsible for perceiving and reacting, what you perceive and react to is the only thing "real" to you, while the outside world is what you give meaning to. Any meaning you give makes sense to you, of course. You have total choice of what you want to perceive and react to. Or, better still, *not* react at all.

Not reacting does not mean that you are passive, but instead it puts you in a position of power. It means that you will gain the power of conscious creation.

You can determine that you want to **act positively**, instead of **reacting negatively** to events, situations or people. You do NOT have to feel the way you feel, if it is causing you harm. You do NOT have to feel lonely, depressed, upset, angry, inferior, ugly, etc. You do NOT have to render yourself a **slave** of your mind but become a **master** of it instead.

When you act, instead of reacting, how you want to feel is totally up to you and not dictated by what's happening "outside".

You choose positively how you want to feel, irrespective of situations, events, or other people. You act from point of power rather than being swayed by how the "outside" would have you feel; the "outside" cannot make you feel bad unless you give it permission to do so. The power of choice is in you and never "outside".

Knowing this, how could it change your life if you were able to perceive events with a higher perspective, instead of blindly reacting to them?

It's possible to feel happy or neutral no matter what happens. And you can start consciously creating what you truly desire, instead of being dictated by "outside" events.

Ultimately, you decide how you want to feel. The moment you realize this, that you have total control over how you feel regardless of the "outside", is the moment of true power. Whatever is in your mind is the reality that you experience, and you have total control over your perceptions and actions.

Once you become master over your own mind, you can generate positive feelings and emotions from the inside, never relying on the outside to bring you happiness and contentment. This is what people mean when they say that happiness can only be found inside of you.

A cultivated mind stops reacting blindly but instead lets things be, with no attachment or clinging, observing feelings as the way they are and acting from a point of power.

With recent advances, scientists discovered on the intellectual level that physical reality does not exist, as we have seen. However, Buddha already experienced the "emptiness" 2,500 years ago and *lived* his life in line with this profound wisdom.

Understanding the nature of physical reality at the intellectual level is the first step towards higher truth for many people but it's only the beginning of a new way of living.

One must keep cultivating the mind and growing at the *experiential* level, the *being* level. True understanding is through **experiencing** and **living** in the wisdom, and it goes way beyond mere intellectual understanding.

You, the mind within the framework of the body, are the creator.

In your mind lies enormous power: the only power that can lead you to where you want to be.

Four Stages of Mental Processing

When the mind processes information from the environment it goes through four stages: sensing, thinking, feeling, and generating emotions.

The most important step in this process is thinking, because a lot of thinking is habitual and subconscious, and it determines the final outcome, your feelings and emotions.

You are going to learn that thinking can be divided into two types, reactive thinking and initiative thinking. You will understand that gaining control over your own thinking is gain control of your own destiny.

When the raw electromagnetic signals are transmitted from the brain to the mind, the first stage of mind processing is sensing. Here in the mind the raw signal from the brain is translated into images.

If you are looking at a beautiful flower, now at the sensing stage you perceive the image of a flower. If you are looking at a flipped middle finger, now you perceive the image of a flipped middle finger.

These images are "raw", you won't feel your breath is taken away by the beautiful flower or angered by the flipping of the middle finger. You see what it IS, there's no added feelings and emotions. An image is an image, that's all.

For easier understanding let's use the metaphor of a coloring book.

At this stage of sensing by the mind you see the raw image of the coloring book. You see the raw patterns on a coloring book, with no colors or anything. It is what it is.

The second stage of information processing within the mind is thinking. What you sensed triggers thought. The thinking process varies greatly among people, and no two persons are the same. Therefore, the thoughts triggered are strikingly different and extremely subtle among each individual.

What thought is triggered is based on your past experiences, preferences, inclinations, personalities and more importantly, your beliefs.

If you see a beautiful flower, at this stage of mind processing you start to associate the image with your past experiences.

Maybe it can trigger a very pleasant memory of you planting flowers with your beloved grandma who you miss so much.

Maybe it reminds you of a person you had a romantic relationship with but broke up with.

Maybe it triggers the thinking of how beautiful nature is.

The thought triggered by sensing can be very subtle and beyond your imagination, it is happening automatically and subconsciously.

In the case of seeing the middle finger flipping, maybe you are thinking how rude that person is who flipped a finger at you.

Maybe it reminds you of your careless youth.

Maybe it made you think people have no patience and tolerance in today's society.

Maybe you feel compassion for the person doing it because you developed unconditional love for humanity.

Or maybe you came from a totally different culture and belief system where flipping the middle finger does not mean something offensive.

The thinking triggered by sensing varies vastly and it really depends on your past experiences and your belief system.

And in this step of mind processing, if the mind is not well-trained the thinking is rather automatic and reactive, you are simply responding to "outer" environments and you don't have conscious control of how you respond; your mind is running on prewritten scripts.

In our coloring book metaphor, the process of thinking is like putting on colors on your coloring book. What color you choose is based on your personal preference and personal choice. Except that the mind "chooses" thoughts more automatically and unconsciously than choosing a color for your coloring book.

Thinking is the most critical stage of mental processing, because not only that it influences the subsequent stages, feelings and emotions, it is also self-reinforcing and self-generating.

Like attracts like. Once a thought is generated it brings about similar thoughts. It's as if you are pulling one pearl on a pearl necklace and all the linked pearls are coming with it. The thought also grows like rolling a snowball, it can massively expand and multiply the sensations. We will come back to this later.

Once the thoughts are generated, the third stage of mental processing is feeling.

Thoughts trigger corresponding feelings. If you see a beautiful flower, at this stage of mind processing you start to have feelings.

In the case where the thought triggered is a very pleasant memory of you planting flowers with your beloved grandma who you miss so much, then the feelings may be missing your grandma.

In the case where the thought is a reminder of a person you loved but broke up with, the feelings triggered might be sadness and regret.

In the case where the thought triggered the thinking of how beautiful nature is, then you may feel deep gratitude of how bountiful and mighty nature is.

In the case of seeing middle finger flipping, if you are thinking how rude that person is who flipped a finger at you, then your feelings might be anger.

In the case it reminds you of your careless youth, perhaps your feeling is sympathy.

If your thought triggered is people have no patience and tolerance in today's society, then you may feel hopeless and disappointment.

If your thought is neutral since you came from a culture where flipping the middle finger doesn't mean anything, then you may feel undisturbed.

In our coloring book metaphor, the process of feeling is like the end result of coloring. Now you have a vivid image. Now your coloring book is colorful.

Since different people choose different colors, they end up with strikingly different results. Some are gloomy, some are inspiring, even if the starting raw pattern is the same.

By the feeling stage of mind processing you have a fully completely art, an art of your unconscious choosing. It's vivid and it's intense.

The feeling stage is fully *internalizing* and receiving the energy that was originally received from "outside" of us. *Feeling is receiving*.

However, since feeling is dependent on how you think, this internalized energy from "outside" is also distorted.

The fourth stage of mind processing is to emote, generating emotions.

To emote is to transmit the energy "outwards" away from us. To emote is to give out, to show your energy for the world to see. It is to allow the energy to complete the cycle and fully flow through you.

Energy cannot be destroyed. It travels, transmits, it comes and goes. It can change from one form to another, but it won't disappear. Generating emotions is to complete this energy flow.

If you see a beautiful flower, at this stage of mind processing you start to show emotions.

In the case where the thought triggered is a very pleasant memory of you planting flowers with your beloved grandma who you miss so much, the corresponding feeling is missing your grandma, then the emotions may be shedding tears.

In the case where the thought is a reminder of a person you loved but broke up with brutally, the feelings triggered might be sadness and regret, the emotions generated might be a deep sigh or frown.

In the case where the thought triggered the thinking of how beautiful nature is, then you may feel deep gratitude of how bountiful and mighty nature is, the emotions might be a wide smile.

In the case of seeing middle finger flipping, if you are thinking how rude that person is who flipped a finger at you, then your feelings might be anger, your emotions may drive you to flip your middle finger back at the person.

In the case it reminds you of your careless youth, perhaps your feeling is sympathy, your emotions may be as subtle as saying to yourself, "I hope this person will change as they grow older".

If your thought triggered is people have no patience and tolerance in today's society, then you may feel hopeless and disappointment, your emotions may lead you to shake your head.

In our coloring book metaphor, the process of generating emotions is like showing your work of art to people. You hold an art show for people to see. Or perhaps you want to hide it because it's not very pretty.

As human beings we are social creatures, we want to show people how we feel by showing our emotions. We want to be sympathized if our feelings are not so great because we don't want to be alone. That's why we are very vocal in spreading our negativities.

If our feelings are good, we are naturally open and want to show our pleasant emotions. Positive emotions are contagious, just like the negative emotions.

In the case of not wanting to show unpleasant emotions because of ego's pride, our emotions still show subconsciously in very subtle ways.

Sometimes it is not socially acceptable to show anger. For example, showing your rage at work in front of your boss, you could be kicked out on the spot. Perhaps you are having marriage issues but don't want others to know. Perhaps it is the fear of financially not being able to get by, but it's not something you can vent out to anybody.

Through social learning, we managed and trained our mind to hide and bury emotions when they're inappropriate to be displayed.

These trapped emotions have to have a place to go, if it's not going outwards it's trapped inside, and it is the body where it goes to.

Each type of emotion carries with it an energy blueprint. Different body parts have different affinities for different emotional energies.

For example, sexual organs store the trapped emotions related to romance. Perhaps it's a crying for intimacy. Perhaps it's anger towards your ex and not being able to let go. Perhaps it's dissatisfaction and not feeling loved. Perhaps it's sexual desire not being answered. These subtle emotions when not being expressed, transformed or let go of, stores in sexual organs and with the buildup may manifest into diseases in corresponding bodily regions. The emotional energy is seeking a way of expression.

Lungs attract the trapped emotions of fear of not being able to live. Have you ever felt lacking hope in life? It felt like you are suffocating, doesn't it? It is essentially the fear of not being able to live. When you have that feeling your breathing subconsciously goes shallower. This type of trapped emotion goes to the lungs.

Since we are not as sensitive to changes and pains in our internal organs as we do to what happens on the surface of our body, such as a cut on the finger or a bruise, these deeply buried emotions go unnoticed for months and years until it generates a massive explosion and manifests into life-threatening diseases.

By the time the bodily malfunctions become detectable, we had long forgot its real cause, deeply buried emotions from long ago. Our mind might had pushed the actual life event that caused that negative emotion deep in the subconscious.

Healing at the emotion level is deeper than at the bodily level since the bodily level is the end result not the cause. You want to get to the root cause of the problem as much as you can because if you simply fix the surface the problem will reoccur, perhaps in a slightly different fashion.

It's like you have a Word document, after you print it out you find out that there's a typo. You cross out the typo with a pen on your printout and write down the correct word without fixing your Word document on your computer.

Next time you print out another copy and find the same error. You get mad and ask why this is happening again even after you fixed it.

That's the type of madness we are doing with healing, we are fixing the surface but not removing the root cause of it.

Channel your emotions, transform them to higher vibrations just a little at a time, and better still let go of them so they can flow out to the Universe and be converted properly.

Healing on the emotional level is a great approach and it has to be done on an individual basis.

There is an even better approach to healing, and that is to eliminate reactive thinking.

I hear you ask, "Are you trying to turn me into a robot?"

My answer to that is of course not!

I mentioned earlier that among the four steps of mind processing, sensing, thinking, feeling, generating emotions, the most critical step is thinking.

Thinking is self-generating and self-reinforcing and automatic process. Our thought process is greatly governed by the subconscious mind. How you think becomes a pattern, it's like a well-traveled dirt road where the two rows of wheel prints are deeply ingrained into the dirt. And every time you travel it's the same tracks you go down. How you think is a habit.

We are unconsciously following the same thinking pattern, as if we are following a prewritten script. We need to make our thinking more conscious and directed to create a new and more beneficial thinking pattern.

Thought attracts like thoughts and it snowballs to multiply the sensations.

Raw sensations are what they are, but unconscious thinking greatly exaggerates the sensations.

If it's a sensation of pain, it's a lot more tolerable without reactive thinking. In vipassana meditation, the attention is focused on the raw sensations. Observe what it is, with no mental attachment, simply watch it come and go. What you are practicing is removing reactive thinking.

Since human beings are complex and rather intelligent creatures, it's not as simple as to keep at the sensation levels. We created language to communicate. Our thinking, feeling and emotions are easily transmitted through words we speak or heard, books we write and read, videos we create or watch, etc. The transmission has no time and space barrier anymore.

Anyone's thinking can be transmitted across the globe and down the history lane as well. Today we are living in a world where fear and panic due to a local killing or virus outbreak can sweep across the globe and even mentally paralyze a nation.

So not only are we navigating through our immediate physical world, we are also living in a very contagious mental world where thought is magnified and transmitted efficiently from one person to the next.

If we don't put a stop on our reactive thinking, we would have no choice of what's in our mind.

If you can cut out the loop at the sensation level, then you will start to become the master of your own mind.

You may ask,

You mean I don't think, feel and generate emotions anymore?
Won't I be bored to death?
Won't I be like a machine?

Thinking can be divided into two types, one is reactive, one is initiative. The reactive type of thinking is passive, you receive information from outside of you then you respond by generating thoughts. It is unconscious and you don't consciously choose how you would like to think; you just run with it and be controlled by your environment.

Thinking is self-generating. Initiative type of thinking is to purposefully create thoughts from within instead of in response to the "outside".

When you no longer react to sensations and simply let it be, you have full control of your own mind. When necessary, you can consciously generate beneficial thoughts.

We have over 3000 thoughts flow through our mind every day. How many of those thoughts are useful? How many of those thoughts are repeating thoughts of not being loved, inadequate, not good enough, cannot get by, not worthy, disappointing, afraid, scarce, and lacking?

What if you stop those thoughts on the tracks and instead initiate thoughts of love, abundance, vitality, worthy, beautiful, bright, cheerful, and joy?

Therefore, put a stop on thinking in reaction to the "outside", instead initiate thinking of your choice from within. When you practice this in the beginning, it may feel like swimming against the current and that is OK. You are getting rid of the old pattern and creating a new thinking habit.

Wallace Wattles said the following:

To think health when surrounded by the appearances of disease, or to think riches when in the midst of appearances of poverty, requires power; but he who acquires this power becomes a Master mind. He can conquer fate; he can have what he wants.

This power can only be acquired by getting hold of the basic fact which is behind all appearances; and that fact is that there is one Thinking Substance, from which and by which all things are made.

Then we must grasp the truth that every thought held in this substance becomes a form, and that man can so impress his thoughts upon it as to cause them to take form and become visible things.

When we realize this, we lose all doubt and fear, for we know that we can create what we want to create; we can get what we want to have, and can become what we want to be.

This is also what meditation teaches.

Meditation is a process of training the mind to achieve the thoughtless state or on top of that initiate thoughts from within with intention. It is training your mind to gain control over your mental focus, not the same old disempowering interpretation of what the environment is telling you.

"We either live with intention or exist by default." - Kristin Armstrong, three-time Olympic gold medalist

Your mind is your great gift, you can either be its slave or be its master. It is about consciously and purposefully choose how you think. This is the pathway to personal power.

Conscious, Subconscious, and the Soul Mind

By now you understand the power of your own mind, and why you need to cultivate and get in touch with it. Now let's take a closer look at the mind itself.

We divide the mind into the conscious mind, the subconscious mind (or unconscious), and the soul mind. The reason we have these different terms is because we think that there are different "divisions" or "levels" of the mind.

We perceive the outside world through the conscious mind. It not only perceives through our five senses, but is also very intelligent, because of the function of reasoning, logic, analysis, judgment, critical thinking, intellect, etc. Think about the mental skills that a mathematician possesses!

Most of the time we identify with our conscious mind, as it's the part that we are most aware of. It's the "you" that you think you are.

The "subconscious" mind sits below our conscious awareness. If the conscious and subconscious mind together is an iceberg, the conscious mind is the visible part above the surface, constituting less than 10 percent of the total mass, while the subconscious is the hidden part below water, accounting for more than 90 percent of the mass.

The functions performed by the subconscious mind seem to be done "automatically" and this partially accounts for our ignorance of its power.

For example, it's responsible for bodily functions such as breathing, heartbeat, subtle sensations of the skin in contact with the clothes, peripheral vision, "background" sound, permanent memories of everything and every feeling that we have ever experienced. It also takes charge of habits, hormonal control, every cellular functioning, and countless other subtle activities that are happening every single second.

In the beginning, when you learn how to drive a car, you must consciously think about where to place your hands and legs. It might feel awkward to switch your foot between the gas pedal and the brake. You have to coordinate all the fine muscles involved and move your body consciously so that you get the hang of it. It seems such a daunting task and you put all your attention to the wheel.

You engage your *conscious* mind to learn this new skill but, soon after you practiced it to get familiar with driving, you no longer need to *think* about it. In fact, you may even make a phone call while driving or munch on a snack while driving. The act of driving had been taken over by your powerful, *subconscious* mind. All the fine body movements and coordination are controlled by your subconscious and performed *automatically*.

This is a simple example of what the subconscious mind does. It also looks after *how* you think. Your thinking pattern or beliefs are taken care of by your powerful subconscious mind, along with anything that becomes a habit. This frees up your conscious mind to focus on unfamiliar tasks or things that command your attention.

While your conscious mind can only deal with a few things at once, your subconscious mind is mastering countless tasks simultaneously without your conscious attention. It is truly remarkable.

The deepest part of the mind, however, is the soul mind. This is where our past life memories and all the feelings that have ever been experienced by our soul are stored, as well as our knowledge of the spirit world.

The soul mind is our true self, our true identity. A person may have acted badly in life because of his or her limiting conscious thinking, but the soul is pure and only knows love.

Whether a person lives his/her true life's purpose depends on how deep the soul is buried. In some people, it could be so deeply buried that they stray away from their true identities and let their real selves suffer inside.

A lot of life's problems have the answer in the soul mind, even though these problems seem rather random on the surface.

Experiences and lessons from past lives propel the soul on its path of enlightenment and understanding the true self. Real enlightenment is measured by how one serves and benefits others; this is elaborated on in later sections.

The Conscious Mind Does Not Exist

Now we understand the different levels of the mind, each takes us deeper to our true identity. However, it first needs to be said that *the division of the mind is artificial*. There are no such divisions, only *perceived divisions*. The conscious mind that we know of *does not even exist*.

I know that it might be hard to accept that the conscious mind does not exist. Let's first use the metaphor of peeking through a small window.

Imagine you are standing outside a huge room from a great distance. This room only has a small window through which to peek inside.

What you see through this window is the content of the conscious mind. Through this window you can see, hear, feel, taste, etc. You also have access to short-term memory, some memories from distant past, and reasoning skills.

Through this tiny window you perceive that this is all there is in the room and you don't question that there may be more. It is enough for you to navigate through physical life.

The entire room is the totality of your mind but, peeking through the tiny window, you are tuned only into the "physical reality" by your physical senses.

There are a lot more interesting and useful contents in the room but, since you are not looking there, you are not aware of them. In fact, the content is so vast that it may overwhelm your conscious mind if you are not ready for it.

Now, at some point you start to awaken and question if what you have seen is all there is, and whether you are missing something important.

You realize that you can easily see the previously unseen part of the room by simply walking closer to the window so that your field of view is larger. Or you can look through a different angle so that some contents previously unseen can be revealed to you when you direct your attention there. If you are looking for something in particular, you can turn towards a particular direction and find what you need.

Such is case with the conscious/subconscious/soul mind. There is no actual division, but it depends on one's focus of attention.

The conscious mind is the window through which you are aware. And content in the "subconscious" and "soul mind" is readily available if you get into the right state of mind to receive it.

The conscious mind directly deals with the physical environment through senses and reasoning abilities. You identify with the conscious mind so much that you don't even question whether or not there is more to what you see.

You might also think of the conscious mind as a telescope. When you see through it you see a tiny spot in the night sky. What you see depends on where you direct it to.

The entire sky is vast and represents the totality of the mind, but we may miss the vast content, depending on our focus.

If we switch the angle of the telescope, we will see another spot of the night sky.

If we enlarge our field of vision, we will then see a larger region including the area that were previously unseen.

The conscious mind is the lens of the telescope through which we become aware.

The conscious mind is not a thing; it is not a division or compartment that is separate from the "deeper" minds but simply a focus of attention, a "focusing" mechanism. Where you focus your attention to, you become aware of it.

When you focus your attention on the deeper minds, it comes to be known to you and enters your conscious awareness. Therefore, what was in the subconscious mind or soul mind can enter your conscious mind, which means you become aware of it.

For most people, this focus is "fixed" on the "outside" world – the physical reality that we know - and we are oblivious to other options.

The most effective ways to bring hidden information to your conscious awareness is through hypnosis and meditation. Hypnosis and meditation is a change of the focus and expansion of consciousness, so that what was previously hidden is brought into focus, your conscious awareness.

The conscious mind, as we have seen, does not exist but for the sake of simple explanation of profound meanings, we will keep using the terms conscious mind, subconscious mind, and soul mind.

What prevents the conscious mind from looking elsewhere?

This is due to its powerful functions of judgement, analysis, intellect, reasoning, and logic, etc. In other words, it locks itself up by its own "intelligence".

Society has developed in the direction of almost entirely relying on facts and evidence. Only things that are tangible, solid, or can be deduced or proven by logic are accepted.

Anything beyond "fact" is ignored, rejected, marginalized, and often scorned. Essentially, only the things that can be understood by the faculties of the conscious mind are accepted as "true".

It's not hard to understand this if you look at the school curricula and consider which professions our societies look up to: doctors, lawyers, etc. Accumulation of knowledge, facts, and logic is overwhelmingly rewarded, while intuition is seen as having no foundation and is actively suppressed in people from a young age.

We are only counting the tip of the iceberg as real while for the over 95% of the part that's submerged in water, we deny its existence. In essence, we are operating with less than 5% of the total of our mental power in our daily lives and ignorant of the rest.

This over-reliance on facts, reasoning, and logic has prevented the possibility of looking into the subconscious and beyond: again, the conscious mind is restricted by its own "intelligence" and not allowed to focus elsewhere but the physical. The point of focus becomes rigid and restricted.

The vastness of the sky is neglected but people are content with what's obviously in front of them, a tiny area of the sky where the telescope is fixed upon. They make the "scientific" conclusion that that's all there is because that's the only thing that can be "proven".

There is nothing unconscious when you direct your consciousness there; the unconscious becomes known and therefore becomes conscious. It's only because we fix our attention outwards to perceive the "outside" world that consciousness seems split.

The conscious mind anchors us to physical reality so that we perceive materials, time, and space the way we do, but we forget that there is no division of the mind and the so-called conscious mind is simply a window through which we observe.

At any time, we can expand this window or look elsewhere so that our field of vision expands. We can find hidden answers to our healing and better our decision-making abilities.

Fortunately, with the discoveries of quantum physics illuminating the energy nature of matter, more and more scientifically orientated individuals are seeing the greater part of reality. Science and spirituality are converging like never before.

Ultimately, the conscious mind will expand to that of the soul mind and that's when true enlightenment is achieved. It is possible for everyone – not only Buddha. We can each become the true embodiment of our soul.

There still is a long way to go. The simple act of accumulating evidences to prove higher realities exist is not enough, we need to move beyond the intellectual level and get to the feeling level of who we really are and how things really work.

The Illusionary False Self - The Ego

Most people identify with their conscious mind. However, remember that it is not a "thing"; it is simply a window through which you focus your awareness.

The conscious mind is intelligent, and it creates a "thing" that enables the conscious mind to feel "beingness". But it is an illusionary being.

We must understand who the "I" is that you identify with so much.

Imagine a big circle, in the middle of which is a small circle. This small circle is "I". This "I" is so important that it must be capitalized. It is so important that you have to defend it, as if "I" holds the only truth. Other people who hold different opinions than "I" are crazy. One could even kill to protect the "I". It is superior to anything labeled with "else" or "others".

Not only is "I" so important but so are its "possessions". Beyond this "I" is the ever-expanding large circle, the my/mine, "possessions" of the "I".

- My house
- My car
- My children
- My family
- My company
- My money

- My tree
- My garden
- My mansion
- My table
- My computer
- My problems

If I accidentally drop a very expensive camera and break it, I start crying. If someone else I don't know drops the same brand of camera and breaks it, "I" don't even care, or I may even laugh.

But who is the "I" really?

Why everything is perceived from the angle of this "I"?

Are other people's "I" as important to them as my "I" to me?

The "I" you identify with is your ego, the "false" self.

The conscious mind constantly looks outwards to the physical reality. It is so intelligent, but also so ignorant of the deeper minds, that it created a "false" self; an imaginary self that it identifies with - the ego.

The ego gives the conscious mind a feeling of "self", "uniqueness", "entity", "being", a sense of "separateness" from other beings and things.

The conscious mind and the ego feed back into each other, reinforcing each other's presence. The ego is fed, made bigger and bigger, while the being strays further and further from its true identity. It does not see the interconnectedness of all beings and things; it only sees its own importance.

The ego fears death, because death will remove the perceived divisions between the conscious mind, subconscious mind, and soul mind, making ego unnecessary.

The so-called conscious mind is only a focus and, when it is no longer confined by physical senses, it expands, and the totality of the mind becomes conscious. Expanding awareness will annihilate the ego and so the ego fears physical death.

Even to lose an argument is seen as the demise for ego, a symbolic death. That's why it will not give in to others or yield in any way. It must "win" the argument to ensure its survival.

To the soul mind, however, there is no death and it is always in the process of becoming.

"I" is the ego that your conscious mind identifies with; it is who you *think* you are. But *are you* who you think you are?

I had a vivid dream one night in which I was playing the role of a woman I had totally identified with. "I" had thoughts and actions, they all felt so real in the dream. "I" was emotionally involved. There was no single doubt during the dream that I was this woman and that this woman was me.

Then I woke up, realizing that it was only a dream. After a little reorientation upon awakening, my sense of "I" slowly came back to normal, the Sue Maisano that I identify with in waking hours.

It was so real within the dream that the woman was me, just not the everyday self I identify with in waking hours. I felt like I switched "I" during the dream and an alien "I" took over. In fact, that "I" from the dream was as real as the "I" in my waking hours.

You see, the identity of the "I" is changeable and expandable as well. It is not the limited personality that we perceive ourselves to be.

When I think back to my distant past, growing up as a Chinese farm girl, "I" was this Chinese girl with the name of Xu Liu.

As a little Chinese girl, I had thoughts, ideas, views, and inspirations that were totally different to those I hold now. "I" now even identify with a totally different name, living here as an American mom. It feels like two different lives, with my distant past feel like a dream.

The "I" had been shifted and expanded.

Look into your own distant past. Are you the same "I" that you identified with before?

Is this sense of "I" changing gradually but constantly?

Is it possible that life itself is a dream?

Like a dream, what if the "I", the ego, you identify with now is not who you really are?

Will there be a time when you wake up, realizing that the "I" you identified with in your life to date is not the actual you?

Who are you when you remove all the self-imposed limitations?

What if you found out that your real identity is so vast that it cannot be named or defined?

What if you experience your true self and realize that it is outside the realm of time and space?

With expanded understanding what would you do differently in life?

Your new journey begins with the understanding of who you really are.

Your True Self - Soul Being

Death is the process of stripping away what's not truly yours, so you are left with only you.

What you have is not what you are; what you are is not what you have. Upon death, you become the real you, totally naked with no belongings, just the raw you, as when you were born.

You can't take your loved ones with you when you die. You can't take your house. You can't take your money. You can't take any of your belongings.

You can't even take your body with you, it will be returned to nature, turned into other forms and recycled. You drop your physical manifestation when you die. You let go of all your belongings including your body, which are not the actual you.

So, what can you take with you? Nothing but yourself. You are returned to your original form, fully liberated from material bonding.

You become the true YOU, the life force, the energy, the essence, the consciousness that is your soul. You drop what you have so you become totally you.

You will be free of bondages; you will be no longer confined by a physical body and plugged in to physical senses.

Upon death, the departing soul is released from the body. It is the time of awakening from a "dream". You realize that the "I" that you identified with is only a narrow sense of perspective but not your real essence.

Your actual being is so vast, so powerful, and so much more than you thought you were while inside a body living a physical life. Your awareness expands.

The seeming "barriers" between the conscious, subconscious and soul mind are dissolved and your consciousness is expanded to the totality of your soul mind. Therefore, you become aware of who you really are, and you can see things from a higher perspective.

You see no boundaries.

Upon awakening from the dream called physical life, your true identity will be revealed to you and you may regret how the "I" identified with a narrow sense of what you really are and created so much misery for yourself and others in physical life.

Your dream self might have committed wrong dos to others or limited your own life experiences out of fear.

However, whatever you learned in this lifetime is your eternal treasure inscribed in your permanent memory. From your new, higher perspective, you understand that there are no mistakes - only lessons.

Life is a learning process. You perceive through a physical body, translating energies into sight, sound, objects, etc.; translating events in the axis of time and 3D objects in the axis of space. All this is set up to create an environment perceived as "real" through a physical body, so that you learn in the best way possible.

Through physical manifestations, you learn that you reap what you sow.

Your soul is like a director of a play. It also assumes the main role in the play. Your life's challenges were deliberately designed by you.

Let's say your soul identity is Mike. In the particular play that you designed, you are Frank. Even though you have a set name, Frank, for this particular play, your stage name will change with each new play. But no matter how many plays you did your true identify is Mike and it doesn't change.

You wrote up the script beforehand, based on your previous plays. For example, if in your previous plays you tended to power over others, you will cause others misery. Now, in this new play, you wrote up scripts so that you experience being over-powered. It is not a punishment for you but simply provides the best learning opportunity for learning through experience. In this way, Mike (you!), learns firsthand that overpowering others is not right, because you now can experience the same unpleasant feelings that you had imposed on others.

What better way to learn than switching your role to that of your subject?

In the role of Frank, you experience situations in which you tend to get overpowered. You identify with Frank so much that you think that's who you are. You went through the up and downs as Frank, totally identifying yourself as Frank because you are such a great actor. You perform so well that you think Frank is who you really are.

When the play is over, you come to realize your true self as Mike and you fully understand how it feels to be overpowered.

As the eternal being called Mike you now gained more wisdom. Therefore, in the future you will not impose this feeling on other beings. Now you can design new plays to perfect the next quality you want to cultivate.

Or perhaps as Frank, acting out the play that you scripted yourself, you lost view of the larger sense of the "real" you because you got so caught up in the play. You are not aware that you designed the play yourself.

Your conscious mind, perceiving the physical reality, has free will – the power to choose. This means that, as Frank, you can make choices that divert from the original script.

Perhaps, as Frank, you turn the situation around and start overpowering others again. When the play is over, you suddenly realize that you strayed away from the purpose of the play and you regret the way you performed.

Guess what you are going to script for your next play? Similar plots to put you in similar situations, hoping to get it right this time around.

This is not a punishment but simply a soul's desire to progress as a being. And it also does not mean that Frank would have to suffer his whole life being overpowered, because as soon as the lesson is learned, there is no more need for the situation. When Frank fully learned the lesson of not overpowering others, by experiencing being overpowered in this case, he will no longer experience such situations.

The moment you **accept** the lessons learned, the purpose of the lesson is already served and therefore you will be released from the bad situation. You can now move on to new lessons.

This is how life works. It's not much different than a dream, a movie, or a play. Life is a stage. And the point is this: through learning by the experience of living a physical life, you purify your soul.

You are, in no sense, a *slave* of the past though neither of your past lives or your past in this lifetime. All life designs are for your highest good to learn and to progress, propelling you towards higher understanding.

People tend to resist the idea that their life's difficulties were lessons for them to grow. Or more frequently they are fighting in the trenches, with the hatred of the situation on the back of their mind. The resistance acts as a block preventing them from accepting the lessons they are learning.

It's worth repeating that the moment you **accept** the lessons learned, the purpose of the lesson (or rather the life design) is already served and therefore you will be released from the bad situation. You can now move on to new lessons.

When your mind is open enough to realize that you are a creator and never a victim, you are released from past bondages.

And, at any time, you can reach out for help from your subconscious mind and soul mind, using the resources that you possess to better your life and those of others around you.

The conscious mind is only a window through which you are aware, remember. When you expand your consciousness, you see the larger sense of life and act from the point of power.

You don't have to wait until you die to see higher truth. In fact, you must assimilate the lessons while still in physical body. Why? Because you would have accomplished a great deal when you accept the necessary lessons while in physical body.

Death itself does not get you out of the challenging situation, nor does it skip you from the necessary lessons awaiting you. It's easier to accomplish the lessons in this current lifetime than postponing it to future lives.

You can choose to awaken now. Now is the best time to awaken to your true self and live life from an expanded point of view. Now is the time to make conscious decisions while tapping into your deeper minds.

Earth is the toughest learning school, if you can transcend physical reality in this lifetime while living through a physical body, it's a big accomplishment of your soul. And the lessons you learned through the awakening process benefits you in lifetimes to come.

Your point of power is right now. You are *never a victim of the past*, because there is no past and time does not exist. Time is another illusion of the conscious mind.

Understanding the illusion of time releases enormous healing power in you, because you will be free of bondages of past lives and any past trauma in this life. It will enable you to create your personal reality with the greatest freedom.

The Illusion of Time - Clock Time is Not "Time"

L ike physical matter, time is another brilliant illusion of the conscious mind.

So-called "time" gives the illusion that it flows smoothly from past to present to future. This feeling of time perceived by the conscious mind is for learning purposes.

Time is the "axis" along which event happens. Because there is a perceived "past" that led to "now", and the "now" to the "future", there is perceived cause and effect at play.

It seems that you get where you are "now" because of what you did in the "past". What type of future you will get depends on what you do "now".

This sense of the continuous "flow" of time as perceived by the mind creates the best environment for the conscious mind to learn important lessons. It is a test ground for getting feedbacks, because it seems that your actions lead you to corresponding consequences over time.

What's better than time for you to learn that you reap what you sow? Without the perception of the existence of "time", living a physical life would be meaningless and you wouldn't be able to learn in the best way possible.

The notion of time, among other concepts, enters our belief systems as a well-accepted definition, without question, and we learn it from a young age.

From a physical standpoint, time seems very real and linear. We progress from infant to teenage years, to adulthood, and to older ages as time passes. It seems that our own "aging" process alone is strong "proof" of time passing.

Time seems to be in constant flow, carrying us from the past to future and we don't normally question its validity.

If time does not exist, you might argue, then how could you explain seasons, years, months, daytime and nighttime?

Aren't they proof of the existence of time?

The sun rises in the morning and sets in the evening. How could one deny the existence of time?

However, there is an important distinction we need to make here: between "clock time" and "time".

Clock time does exist, as a method we developed to measure what we think of as "time". The measurement itself solidifies our illusion of time.

However, how we measure time is based on rhythmic planetary movements.

The essence of planetary movement is *change*, or some call it *motion*. Everything is in constant flow of change; every single moment is different to any other.

But change is not the actual time and there is no time, only change; rhythmic change.

A year is defined by the duration taken by a planet, such as Earth, to make one revolution around the sun.

A day is defined by the duration that the planet, such as Earth, spins on its axis and makes one full self-rotation.

Then this self-rotation is used to "calibrate" what we know as clock time because it is divided into 24 segments we call "hours", which are divided into 60 minutes, then a minute into 60 seconds.

The planetary movement is actually constant rhythmic change of position and this change is used to measure what we know as clock time.

The "time" we know of is man-made for convenience. It does not mean that "time" exists.

The Illusion of Time – "Past" and "Future" Are Not "Time"

W e always see time drawn as a line in history books. We were conditioned and fooled by our own mind that time is like a trail - and we follow this trail to go to the future.

We might equate time with the existence of the past or future, thinking that, since there is past and future, there must be time.

However, the so-called "past" comes to our mind as memories and our future as our imaginations within the mind.

Past and future are only "realities" created by the **mind**; they are nothing but illusions. Therefore, "past" and "future" are not proof that "time" exists.

Past and future are mental projections into the moment of "now".

When you think of a past unpleasant experience, for example, you may feel guilty or the inability to forgive someone. You are bringing mental pictures into your mind and recreating the experience in the present moment.

Since your emotions follow your imagination, when you think of the past, it is real in your imagination; you create the same emotions, hormones and physiological conditions that match the experience.

You think you are thinking of the past, but in fact there is no past; instead, you are recreating a feeling that you experienced before in your mind and body in the present.

You never physically go back to the "past"; you simply change your state of NOW to match your past mental state. A mental state you had experienced before entered your awareness at this moment of NOW.

When your mind is projected to the past, which is simply a re-creation of a former mental condition, often painful past feelings, it is impossible to fully engage in the present. That is the reason why so many people "look without seeing", because their mind is not really there with them.

You cannot fully appreciate the beauty of the flower in front of you if your mind is busy with something else imaginary but unpleasant.

Your mind cannot tell the difference between your sensory input and your imagination, they are equally real to your mind. Sensory input and imagination are made of the same thinking substance. They hold the same validity to the mind.

There is really nothing "out there", your sensory input has to be interpreted by your mind to be **perceived**. This process of mind perception makes no difference between perceiving something physically real "out there" or imagination. Sensory perception and imagination are both mind creations; they are equally real to the mind.

Similarly, when you think of the future, often times you are thinking about potential undesirable outcomes, bad things you fear that could happen or things that could go wrong. It is the obsession of the mind to dwell on negative things, whether imagined, past events or the future.

The mind does not like to be idle or be still, it wants to be busy, and past bad memories or future potential disasters give the mind work to do.

The future exists as possibilities; it is not set in stone. You could draw/manifest different possibilities of the future into the present moment.

When you dwell on a negative possibility by worrying about the future, you are mentally projecting and bringing about the corresponding emotions, feelings, and physiological conditions to the present moment.

Since you are tuning to a negative energy by thinking of potential disasters that might happen in the future, you will indeed attract that future possibility into existence, since you are a good match to it.

The law of attraction is a strong force that never fails, even though you could be as oblivious to it as you are to gravity. The only thing that really does exist, what's in the present moment, was neglected and replaced with unnecessary worries instead.

Time is an illusion. ***NOW is the only time you have***. The past was many moments of NOW that you have already experienced, and they exist in your mind as memories that you can bring to your NOW at any time. The future is things that could happen and when they happen, they occur in the form of NOW.

Any time you tune in to the past or future, you are not living in the NOW that you are actually facing. You are mentally projecting to illusions and bringing them to the now. The past and future are realities only in the mind; they are mind creations.

Dwelling on the past or future simply puts you in certain frames of mind in the present moment, but you are never physically out of the moment of NOW.

"Past" and "future" are mind creations; they are simply illusions. They are not proof that time exists.

So, remember that NOW is the only "time" you have, and it is the only "time" that you can apply your power.

"Time" is Constant Change: Now is All You Have

Imagine that you are sitting in a car. This car is constantly in motion, not necessarily driving in a straight line, but it never stops moving.

In this metaphor, this car is called the moment of "NOW". You are sitting in this car of "NOW" and you can never physically get out of it.

Inside this car, there is a screen and you are using a video camera to capture what is happening on this screen. The screen is showing constantly changing patterns, with the same scene never shown twice.

What's happening on the screen represents your actual life events, and the video camera is your mind in this metaphor.

You are never dealing with your life events as is, you always do it through the filtering of your mind. You are using your mind to record/perceive events. Therefore, your perception of physical reality together with your life events are mind creations at all times.

Everything you perceive is through your mind, and your mind only. In the metaphor above, your mind is the video camera you are using to capture what's happening on the screen.

The position of the car is in constant change, and what's showing on the screen is also constantly changing. Therefore, what's on the screen is only relevant to the corresponding position of the car and it only happens once. The patterns on the screen is nonrepeating. Once gone, it's gone, with no trace or anything. But of course, your video camera records it and you can rewind to see past patterns if you choose to.

From position A to B, a lot of things appeared on the screen as you recorded them with your video camera. Let's say you are on position B now. You can draw a line, not necessarily straight, between A and B to cover the actual path you traveled and say that this is the time passed and A was your past.

However, the path itself is not relevant since you could have traveled many different paths from point A and still get to point B, your current position. You had many other choices of paths that would also get you to B, which is the most important point right now.

In other words, studying the path itself does not change a thing; it is useless to focus on the path itself.

You may not agree and look up your past recordings and say, "see this is what happened, this is my past". However, what is shown on the screen only happens once and it is only meaningful in relation to the position of the car. Once you moved out of position A, what happened on the screen at that point is no longer there; it was only meaningful when at position A. Once you moved from there, you can only access that scene through your recordings/mind, that means that past only exists in your mind. Past is mind created illusion; past does not exist in the current physical reality.

Each person's video camera is different in very subtle ways. Perhaps the lens colors are slightly different, the size of the recordings vary, or there are other subtleties. Therefore, when you look through your video camera recordings, you are not looking at the ACTUAL reality on the screen; it's a representation of what happened but never the real thing.

The "real" thing does not exist anymore since the car moved out of that "past" spot. What shows on the screen is only real when the car is at the corresponding position when it happened. When you look at the recordings to view what happened at point A, the so-called past, you are doing so from point B, your current position.

Importantly, while you go and check your video recordings of point A you miss the chance to record what is happening "now" on the screen at point B.

All that you are doing is looking at a mental recording of what happened and equating that to what actually happened but that no longer exists and never again will exist. The "past" is gone forever and is irrelevant now. Only the mind makes it real and persist and become obsessed with it.

Time not existing does not mean that past events and happenings were not real. They were real at the very moment when they occurred, and they were only **relevant** at that moment. Once the moment passed, they were no longer real; because they do not exist anymore. The only thing that makes them real is your mind.

What happened to the "past" events that were so real back then?

Where are they now?

What happened is **change**.

They changed, they evolved to the events at the present moment. All that there is is **CHANGE**; everything is in motion and there is no **trace** left. Time, as we know it, only exists in the conscious mind.

For example, there is no child version of you, a teenage you, a young adult you, then the you of the present, now. There is only one you and it is changing, constantly changing. Because of the continuous change, you have a completely different body than the you of 20 years ago, but it does not mean there are two of you; you have simply CHANGED.

Past events, like people, do not leave any trace or stay in the "past", but simply change and evolve to new states.

You registered events and happenings in your mind; but what's in the mind is not reality itself. The past is passed and can no longer affect you now, because it was only relevant at its own "now" and this no longer exists.

There is only never-ending change and this process of changing creates an illusion in the conscious mind of "time" passing.

Why would the mind create the illusion of time?

The conscious mind creates the feeling of "time" to organize happenings in a perceived sequence and seemingly cause and effect.

Time is a creation of the conscious mind for learning purposes.

Understanding that time does not exist can bring great healing power. The past can no longer drag you down or hold you back and the future can no longer make you worry.

Past abuses, poverty, injustice, torture, sufferings are already gone for good. Only when you allow it to affect you will it be able to, by allowing your mind to create that horrible reality for you at the moment of now.

Letting go of the bondages of the past and future is your choice, and you choose powerfully. You are not shackled by any past moments; in every single second, you are reborn and totally free.

The Illusion of Time: Change Your "Past" or "Future" to Benefit Your NOW

Since time does not exist, you can change your past as easily as you change your future.

Most people agree that they can change their future because it hasn't come yet but cannot accept the idea of changing the past since it is generally considered to be a "factual" series of events already happened.

When you consider both the past and future as imaginations in the mind, it changes everything.

Looking into the future, we understand that it is only an imagination and we have the power to change things. Let's say that you are 40 now. When you were 10, all that was real was the moment of "now" happening 30 years ago; everything else was imagination.

At that young age, you might have had vivid thoughts about what you wanted to become when you are 40, but it's only a mind projection; nothing but an imagined reality. More likely than not, that imagined reality does not match your current situation, which you are experiencing for real now at age 40.

We accept easily that the childhood idea formed about the 40-year-old you was not real.

Similarly, the image of that 10-year old you have in your mind now is also a mind projection, an *imagined past*. The only difference is that you now have "memory" as a "proof" of the things that happened along the way. It seems that your **imagination** of the so-called past is validated by physical "reality".

Future exists as possibilities. You are always making choices. The choice you make now out of the possibilities will determine your future path. In other words, you easily understand that you can change your future by making choices now.

But, similarly, what happened in the past was only a possibility from the standpoint of an even earlier time point. In other words, all your past experiences were possibilities at one point and manifested into the physical existence.

The biggest effect of the "fact" that did happen, out of many possibilities in the past, is that it registered in your mind, and you take what's in your mind as "real": the actual thing that exists. Other possibilities were abandoned, and the mind tightly gripped onto the so called "fact" and therefore keep letting the "fact" affecting the subsequent choices. In other words, you subject your now and future to the "past", and that's why you are creating reality at a *liner* fashion. You allow your past to keep haunting you and dictating your now and your future. That's why you are stuck where you are.

Why project your mind in one direction (the future) and accept that it is an imagined reality, yet deny the same when projected in the other direction (the past), believing it is fixed and real because you "experienced" it?

Why feel that you cannot change it because it is a "fact"?

Why take the past so seriously in your mind and allow it to confine and limit your choices now?

You can change your past just as easily as you can change your future. Remember that only what you are experiencing right now is real, while mind projections out of the now, either seemingly forward to the future or backwards to the past, are imagined realities. And you can certainly change what you imagine.

The absolute "reality" of what happened back then will not change, but all the colorings can be altered, and you can gain new interpretations that are more beneficial for you now. The absolute reality of the past does not matter now anyway, because:

1) Once it's happened, it's gone forever;
2) There is no absolute reality anyway - only "reality" perceived by the *mind*;
3) You perpetuate the past and give it power only within your mind. It has no effect unless your mind makes it so.

Your mind is all you need to change in order to change your past, since the past is nothing but an imagined reality in your mind.

When you give a different meaning to past events, situations, or feelings, you have already changed the impact of the past on you at the present moment.

Not only that, all subsequent events, situations, or feelings that are relevant to the initial past event will also change accordingly.

It would be as if the initial event happened differently or as if you had expanded understanding back then.

All you need to do is to mentally release yourself from the perceived hurt from the illusionary past.

When an initial event that is bothering you is viewed with expanded awareness, with the higher understanding that you possess now but lacked when it happened, the coloring of the event will change. You get "unstuck", empowered, and can start to heal. It makes no difference if the past event had happened differently in the first place. The effect is the same: you change your past, and more importantly you change your now.

You are in the car of "now" and events are happening only "now" too. There is no trace left behind the car, only imaginary ones. It is silly to focus on an imaginary trace of how you get to where you are now, because, once you pass the spot, it's no longer there. You could have drawn imagined paths and they are equally valid.

There could be many other possible ways to get to where you are now other than the one you registered in your mind. Letting the "past" affect you in a negative way is simply fooling yourself!

Since the past is only an imagined reality in the mind, does it matter if you imagine it one way or the other? How would you like to change your past?

You can imagine that things had happened differently to your own favor for example. Your "altered" past and the past that did actually happen are equally valid when perceived from the moment of now because they are both imaginations by the mind.

Some people use the term Multiverse and say that the past possibilities that did not actualize were still happening in an alternative reality. You can understand it that way if it is helpful for you to redesign your past.

Feed energy to an alternative past that's more beneficial for you now, set this as the actual past that indeed happen instead of a painful past. As long as you can change your mind and let go of a traumatic past, that's all that matters.

Your past and future are both at your disposal. Do not let your past dictate your future. In every moment of now, you are totally reborn whether you know it or not. Cherish your reborn opportunities, don't choose to be reborn to the same old person with the same old limitations. Allow yourself to be reborn in a magnificent way!

Understanding the illusion of time provides a logical standpoint for allowing letting go to happen, but we need to move beyond logical level and really feel the illusion of time and how it affects our lives. Cultivating higher understanding of the nature of mind reality allows true healing to occur.

The Illusion of Time: How to Benefit Yourself in Conscious Creation

We know that past and future are not real, that time does not exist, and the moment of now is all we have. The present moment is your only point of power. The past and future are irrelevant and dwelling on them will disturb your "now", where your true power lies.

The reason why every individual is at his/her current position is not because of their "past" but because of the choices they make at each moment of "now". Using the past as an excuse is due to ignorance of the choices that you have right "now".

If you allow your past choices dictate the choices you have now, you sure will limit what you are capable of. Let go of the trap of the so-called past. Your point of power lies in the present moment and every individual has *equal* opportunity, regardless of their "past".

You might say "but my 'now' is so painful that I want to escape".

There is no escape; there is nothing to escape from and nowhere to escape to.

The events and happenings of now are **impersonal**; there are no good or bad, only what the mind interprets them to be.

So, the only thing you can do is to change your mind, expand your consciousness, and cultivate your higher understanding. Then

THE NATURE OF MIND REALITIES

you will find that there are no problems in the "now". There are only problems when the mind projects to the illusionary past or future.

While your mind perceives things, it is really filtered perceptions; you never see absolute reality because there is only what the mind *perceives* as reality and each mind and its history is different. Therefore, even the same event is interpreted differently by different people, sensing and filtering the experience through their own minds.

So what is really happening has no good or bad; it is neutral and impersonal. If the human mind can grasp this, then there is no misery or pain whatsoever to escape from.

If you can face your mind now, the present moment becomes enjoyable and you will no longer be seeking that false sense of escape from your present.

When you live in the moment of now to the fullest, you make the best of "time" and you shatter the shackles of the past and future. This is where deep healing starts, and you begin to empower yourself.

Time is perceived as linear by the conscious mind, as a means for our higher self to learn cause and effect. If you can learn exponentially in a period of time you gain time exponentially.

We all have the feeling sometimes that time flies when you are happy but when you are feeling down it is gruelingly slow. Time is highly subjective.

Sometimes you feel it's extended, and other times shortened because time is a creation of the mind.

When you are engrossed in whatever you are doing and are mentally present at the task in hand, you might feel the slowing down of time in each moment and feel the stillness of time. In the end, you might be amazed that quite some time, clock time, has passed. We may not live in the same "psychological time" even though the clock says we share the same time.

Time is an illusion! But can you use this illusion to your advantage? Absolutely!

Engage in activities that foster your learning. Go on a vacation, attend a yoga class, set up a date with your loved one, perform art or music, or simply do something fun that takes you out of your daily routine. Enjoy spontaneity sometimes and go with the flow.

Do things that inspire you and lift you out of your daily grind, such as enjoying nature, gardening, learning about the cosmos, or things that allow you to expand your perspective and feel the vastness of the Universe. The mental representations of such activities are larger than linear time could explain, and you build lasting memories that "extend" time.

When dealing with negative feelings from the past, release the pain by acknowledging that the past only exists in your mind and you choose to let it go. The memory will still be there, but its negative effects and "coloring" will be gone, and you will no longer be a victim of it.

Since the past is only real in the mind, you can purposely use the illusion of time to bring about feelings of content, confidence, love, and compassion to your present moment.

For example, you can choose to tune into and relive a past moment where you succeeded in an endeavor and bring that feeling of confidence and success to your present; this may be beneficial in overcoming a challenge you are now facing. Your positive emotions will follow your imagination and you will gain confidence naturally from the inside.

Consider your past experience as your "treasure" where "bad" feelings are neutralized, let go of, or drawn upon for valuable lessons. Meanwhile you can use good feelings from the past are a resource you can tune in for power at any time.

Many people, who do not understand the illusion of time, unknowingly "fix" their future in a negative way.

The uncultivated mind tends to worry about undesirable future possibilities, unwanted things happening, or desirable things not happening.

The mental projection is so strong that it blocks off all other possibilities and deliberately seeks out the potential disaster. They may say "Oh, it's beyond my power to change it". But they don't even try, preferring to focus on future worries.

Don't allow yourself to live in this horrible, mind-projected future, where your emotions follow your imagination and you end up creating the "feeling patterns" that match the potential pitiful outcome. The reality you experience is the reality created in your mind and you close yourself off to other possibilities, fixing the future on the one that you fear.

How is this likely to turn out? You get the exact thing that you feared. On one level, you are happy because you now can say "See! My worry was justified!".

People who live like this continue to "fix" the future unconsciously while denying their own creative power.

Just as remembering a past event can put your mind in that past mental state now, imagining a potential negative outcome in the future renders your mind in the corresponding state in the present moment of now.

As quantum mechanics show us, observation affects reality. When being observed, the quantum particles cease to be in a state of probability waves but become "fixed" particles.

Likewise, your awareness "fixes" possible realities. Where you put your attention to is what you are going to get: that's your creative power. An uncultivated mind uses their creative power just as strongly, in the wrong direction.

To create a desirable future, consciously train your mind to think about positive outcomes for each endeavor. Bring that "success moment" in the future to the present moment and live in it fully, just as you tune in to past good feelings.

With a favorable imagined result in the "future", you bring your current state to a higher vibration, the same mental state as when your desired outcome arrives. By the law of attraction, with this higher vibration, you will draw the favorable future into your present moment because you are constantly "fixing" possibilities into solid particles.

The way you create is by choosing, and you choose with your thoughts in the moment of now.

Understand the illusion of time and use it at your advantage for conscious creation. "Time" comes to you and flows through you while you are always in the eternal here and now.

If your mind is present at each moment, then you get the most out of "time". You are growing older not because of time but because of change. If you slow down your change, then you will look "younger" than your age, which is measured merely by clock time.

Time is *change*. Accept that things are changing and don't be attached to any change, be it a beautiful or painful moment from the past or potential success or "failure" of the future; whatever it is, it will "change".

Always live in the moment to the fullest. Letting go and non-attachment is a great way of living. It stills your mind and slows down change.

Understanding the illusion of time helps you let go and has the power to bring peace and harmony into your daily life. The importance of mindfulness or "living in the moment" has been recognized since ancient times, and indeed it has profound meanings beyond scientific measure.

At the moment of now, the only real "time", try to bring all your senses to the present and you will cultivate feelings of contentment and harmony.

When you walk, feel your muscles move in perfect harmony; when you eat, feel the flavor and the contact of the food in your mouth; when you look around you, observe the fine details that would otherwise escape you.

At every moment, try to fully experience what's going on now with your senses, with no attachment to the moment prior or the next.

When you are fully present, there are no worries or fear. All you have is peace and harmony right now and forever.

Misunderstanding time is the foundation for many ailments and other miseries in life. If you break free the illusion of time and start living to the fullest in the present moment, you can use time to your advantage and empower yourself to create your chosen personal reality. It will take you to new realms you never knew existed.

Conscious Creation, Letting Go of Reasoning and Logic

With the understanding that time is an illusion, you are released from the bondages of the past and future, and you create your reality with freedom.

You create your reality at each moment. Your conscious creation starts with your deliberate conscious thinking; it is a collaboration between your conscious and subconscious minds.

The power of the conscious mind lies in its focusing and directing abilities, while the power of the subconscious mind is in carrying out orders faithfully and doing the actual work without the need to "micromanage"!

Think of the conscious mind as the CEO of a company. He is the face of the organization and deals with many important matters, organizing press conferences, signing new deals, etc.

Within his company there are many other functions that are very important too, such as product development, customer service, sales and marketing, finance, public relations, etc. These departments are all experts in their own areas, and get their jobs done efficiently without the need for the CEO to micromanage.

For example, the CEO getting involved in paying the monthly bills to suppliers is unnecessary and could interfere with the daily work of the finance department. Additionally, this would distract the CEO from applying his directing power.

On the other hand, if the CEO finds that something's really not right with a particular department, he can investigate the cause of the problem.

The conscious mind is the CEO and the departments doing the various important "internal" jobs represent the subconscious mind.

With conscious creation, the conscious mind (CEO) gives commands and the subconscious mind (departments) carries out the orders and brings things to actuality.

In order to apply conscious creation, you do not need to understand the nuances of how it works. Gravity works whether or not you consciously understand it. In fact, no one fully understands how and why gravity works, but everyone operates under the laws of gravity, knowingly or not. Likewise, the process of conscious creation works with you knowing it or not.

It is a function of the conscious mind to reason, judge, analyze, dispute, think logically, etc. The conscious mind wants to know "why". But creation itself is beyond the conscious reasoning. Therefore, reason and analysis are not sufficient to create what you want. In fact, it may get in the way.

What you need most is not a complete understanding of why and how it works but simply trust: trust in the power of your mind and trust in the process of creation.

The why and how will be taken care of and may be beyond your conscious understanding. Placing high value on trust also eliminates self-doubt and criticism, which are the biggest obstacles to conscious creation.

When you use reasoning and judgement to explain why and how things *should* happen, you will find that you limit yourself. Your conscious mind can only come up with limited ways of how things can happen, based on your past experiences or things in your conscious awareness, while creation uses all sources from the Universe, fathomable and unfathomable.

It may surprise you how things may happen, or it may appear to be "coincidence", "a miracle" or pure "magic". The "you" in the deeper sense simply knows how to achieve the things your conscious mind desires.

What you need to do is to initiate with your conscious mind and then observe and allow it to actualize. You are the CEO and you must direct without micromanaging. Do not get in the way of creation. Use the power of the conscious mind where it is supposed to be used: to give directions and commands and let the other parts of you that perform the tasks do their jobs with no impediments.

Generate the feelings inside as if your goal has already been achieved; use as many of your sensory modalities as you can to imagine your desired outcome.

Say it's a new car that you want. Use your mind's eyes to see yourself sit in the car holding the steering wheel. Smell the new car scent. Touch the seat and feel the texture of the seat. Hear the surround sound coming from the car's built-in audio. Feel into the feeling of thrill of owning your dream car.

In this example, you firmly state what you want, which is your dream car. Then you tune into the feeling of it already happened/happening.

Your mind cannot differentiate imagination from real time sensory perceptions. Thoughts, either it's a responsive thought to your outer environment or creative thought out of sheer imagination are made from the same thinking substance. They hold the same reality in the mind.

On a deeper level, isn't physical sensing an illusion anyways? Isn't it a mind creation/imagination out of pools of energies? Perception and imagination are intertwined; they are both mind creations.

Therefore, to your mind you already owned your dream car when you visualize it in your mind with absolute faith without self-doubt. You are tuning into the state of being when your goal is achieved. You are mentally there, no different than you actually own the car already.

By using your imagination, you are simply collapsing "possibilities" into "fixed particles" just as conscious observation fix quantum particles from probability waves into particles.

Please notice that this is not about fooling your mind to believe something that does not exist. If it feels like you are fooling yourself, that means that you do not yet truly believe you can achieve what you desire. This is a huge block for many people. They do the imagination with doubt in their subconscious mind. Their deep-rooted disbelief is counteracting their manifestation. You need to work on resolving self-doubt to the point you can accept/allow your dream reality as a possibility.

Do not dictate **how** exactly your goal will be achieved, because that will restrict other possible ways for it to happen.

Take it for granted that your goal is ALREADY achieved. You are tuning into the feeling of success, not your journey to it.

Self-doubt is your biggest enemy.

Often times, doubt is created under the guise of logic: "because of this and this, I can't achieve my goal".

Because I don't have money, how can I go on a vacation?

Because I don't have a college degree, how can I find a decent job?

Because I don't have time for the gym, how can I lose weight?

The list goes on and go. This type of linear, logical thinking keeps us stuck where we are currently. It weights us down to the ground without flying up high. With this mentality we won't reach our full potential. We have endless possibilities beyond measure, but they won't be possibilities until your mind opens up to them.

Do not concern yourself with the how, simply take the small first step towards your goal with the faith that you are destined to achieve it. The wonderful feeling you practiced through imagination of your future success is your blueprint and inner GPS, it will help guide you on the journey and manifest the how.

In a model where we feed our mind with things outside of us such as our current environment and our existing situations, it will not carry us to our dreams.

Without detachment to our current limitations we cannot create a new more exciting future. So, detach from your current situation and use imagination to create a new reality from deep within you. Have faith in this new reality.

Faith means you don't need to see physical evidence in order to believe. Faith is beyond conscious thinking and logic.

Whenever you find yourself thinking logically and confining yourself, remind yourself that the CEO is micromanaging and has got in the way of creation.

Reasoning and logic will take you to the next step in a linear way based on your past, therefore, what you can create is very limited when relying solely on reasoning and logic.

There is no limit when you use imagination; the only limitations are self-imposed. The Universe has infinite possibilities and it can bring things to you in surprising ways beyond conscious understanding. Learn how to use your imagination freely again, like a child.

Let's say that your goal is to get to your destination, point B from point A. In scenario one you already arrived. At point B, what're your dominant thoughts?

Will you still be constantly analyzing and worrying about how you can get to your destination or will you be celebrating your arrival to point B and enjoy it to the fullest?

Of course, you would be living from the standpoint of point B, celebrating and living in the thrill filled with gratitude.

In this scenario, which we'll call scenario one, your dream/goal was already achieved, and you have the feeling of excitement and accomplishment.

Now, consider that you have the same goal of going from point A to point B, but you are still in the process of creation. In other words, you are still on the journey from point A to point B. Let's call this scenario two.

In scenario two, should you look at your situation and worry that you may not be able to get to point B? Or can you match your feelings and emotional states to that of scenario one where you already arrived?

Since you are still on the journey of manifestation, you may feel justified to worry that you may never accomplish the goal. Tuning in to the exact feelings of arriving to your destination, which means success, requires a lot more mental and emotional energy.

Getting there mentally before you even embark on your journey will make the journey more pleasant and more likely to succeed. The tug of war of self-doubt will prevent you from accomplishing your goal.

Many people worry because that's their subconscious patterning.

With our knowledge about quantum physics, we understand that our observation creates reality by collapsing possibilities into a definite state. The feeling of fear and worry creates the corresponding results. A positive attitude creates a better outcome. It is a self-fulfilling prophecy.

With imagination, the more you match your feelings to those when the goal is achieved without self-doubt, the sooner you can manifest your goal. That's because the outer is a reflection of the inner. Success is more of a mental journey.

When your inner state changes, so will the outer; and the speed of the change depends on the match of your energy, feelings, and emotions, to that of when the desired outcome is achieved.

The problem with most people is that they are feeding their mind with physical reality, with what's already out there. If the situation is harsh, they are stressed. If the situation is good, then they are happy. Their inner state is a mirror of the outer. This is putting the cart before the horse. Such persons are not creators but slaves. Conscious creation works the other way around. You determine how you would like to feel, then you project that energy outwards, you observe the outer change. This is the creator mode.

It is not an easy task as you can tell. It's somewhat against what we had been taught growing up. I agree that it is indeed an "unlearning" process, and it takes a lot of practice.

You determine the change of your reality and with the power of imagination your conscious creation and achievement has no limitations.

Not only should you not hamper the process of creation itself with the conscious mind's reasoning, logic, or doubt; you should let go of the confinements of the conscious mind when making your goal of creation.

For example, if you make $2000 a month, reasoning and logic will tell you that making $3000 a month is good. Therefore, you are afraid to ask for more or it won't even cross your mind to ask for more.

Since conscious creation does not depend on logic and reasoning, using logic and reasoning to decide what you can create will impose limitations on your abilities. Therefore, you need to get out of the boundaries set up by your own conscious mind and practice to think freely.

The conscious mind thinks in a linear fashion, where things are reasonable and logical. But, to achieve something great, which you are meant to be, something drastically different to your current physical situation, you need to escape the confinement of what you consciously think is possible to achieve.

What you can create is not limited by reasoning, judgment and logic, as you are not solving a math problem. Your creative power is boundless, and the only boundary is the one you put up yourself. Remember that the process of creation is nonlinear. Therefore, break free from the confining liner thinking pattern!

Often times, people dare not navigate beyond their perceived limitations, and these are self-imposed by their own belief systems. Beliefs form the boundaries within which you create your personal reality.

Beliefs: The Boundaries Within Which You Create Your Personal Reality

A belief is an acceptance that a statement is true, or something exists. A belief is a strong conviction in the mind and, because it is held deeply in the mind, it is the "truth" that the mind perceives.

We are talking about belief in its broad sense here; not just religion but about all aspects of life.

Whatever the mind believes, that's the reality you experience. People tend to take their own belief, no matter how distorted it is, as the only truth; everyone else should abide by it. This is what causes wars and other disputes - people defending their rigid beliefs.

All your thoughts and behaviors are within the boundaries of your beliefs. You say and do things within the confinement of your beliefs and you may become oblivious to this fact.

You can't look at the whole picture because you are inside the frame yourself! Beliefs form the frame within which you create your own picture called "reality".

It is like we are trapped within different enclosures. One enclosure is religious belief, another is politics, nationality, race, culture, and so on. The enclosure seems so real for us inside. We don't see beyond these enclosures because we don't know that it is possible to and we forget that we formed our own enclosures in the first place.

If you believe in poverty, then you are very frugal and always in fear of not getting by. You would not reach out to opportunity when it arrives since you believe that, no matter what you do, you will be poor. You become oblivious to opportunities. And indeed, that's the reality you are going to get; it's a perfect match of your mind reality, which is held together with your beliefs.

If you believe in ill health, then you are powerless in the face of disease and relinquish the power of the body's natural healing ability. If you believe that you are not worthy, then you will talk and behave with a lack of self-confidence and your physical reality will be a perfect mirror of this, because you act out what you believe. You manifest outwards what you believe inside.

You hold certain beliefs, and because of these, you act in certain ways. Because you act in certain ways, you get certain results, which confirms your beliefs, of course. It is a self-fulfilling prophecy!

We are never dealing with the absolute physical reality since there is none; remember that we are always viewing realities through the filter of our mind shaped by our beliefs.

It's as if each one of us is viewing the world through invisible internal glasses, each pair different to the next. The colors filtered, the enlargement or shrinking of images, the texture of images, and countless other subtle differences in our internal metaphorical glasses make our views extremely diverse. In fact, no two people have exactly the same beliefs.

Imagine that we are all wearing our own glasses, not externally, but internally in the mind. Each mind "filters" the outside world differently, but unknowingly, because of these different glasses. Your physical reality matches your inner beliefs. What you believe is what you see, because reality is filtered through your own mind.

The question is: who put the metaphorical glasses on us?

As a new-born growing into a young child and then an adult, you are exposed to parents, guardians, teachers, and friends. You watched the TV, read newspapers, browsed social media, read books, and followed different authorities. With their subtle influence, you adopt views, opinions, cultures, and beliefs. So, the answer to the question is: you put the glasses on yourself unknowingly, and start filtering the world.

I had such a startling feeling one day, after communicating with a college friend of mine. Since I left China right after college, I had not been exposed to Chinese culture much for a whole decade. Of course, things have kept evolving in China and everywhere else in the world.

When my friend used a new trendy Chinese term to describe dating, I didn't have a clue what she was talking about. Even after I learned about the word, it still felt awkward to use it, as if it had no meaning to me. I felt at that moment that what you are exposed to shapes your consciousness, and you put yourself in corresponding "enclosures" and keep building upon it. For people inside this enclosure, it makes perfect sense but, to those outside, it has little meaning.

Beliefs work the same way. Each one of us has exposures to different concepts and ideas and we place our attention there, merging our consciousness with them and deciding to accept or reject them.

Each one of us is "shaped" differently by the types of ideas we are exposed to. When you were young, you "set up" your filters unconsciously. Everything you were exposed to was new to you and you did not have anything to compare it to yet; nor could you distinguish the ideas as being helpful or not. You were like a sponge soaking up whatever came along.

This soaking up belief process happens so early, since while we were in the womb until the age of around seven, and it was taking place so subtly that we were not even aware that it was happening.

As we were developing, we observe people around us. From our environment we draw conclusions about ourselves and define who we are and what we are capable of.

By around the age of seven, we had been introduced to the major ideas of how worthy we are, how lovable we are, what is possible or not, how relationships should look like, what money is, how much money makes sense, how hard life is.

Once a belief is formed, it filters ideas you are subsequently exposed to. Things that fit with your existing beliefs are assimilated and it strengthens your beliefs, while those in conflict are discarded. You behave like a filter and this limits your thoughts and behaviors.

We enter our different "enclosures" unconsciously. The enclosures you enter depends heavily on those you were exposed to early on in life. However, this does not mean that belief is a bad thing.

Setting up beliefs is an efficient and convenient way for the mind to cope with the world. With beliefs in place, you have barriers. You don't need to spend unnecessary energy each and every time you come across similar concepts and ideas; you can quickly make decisions to agree or disagree.

Can you imagine yourself changing your mind every single second? Beliefs set up the framework within which you create your personal realities. With the boundaries in place, you can easily navigate without hesitation.

Beliefs are not a problem. They're only trouble when you are restricted by them.

When you are conscious enough, you have the option of examining your existing beliefs, strengthening those that are beneficial to you and abandoning those that are not serving you.

When you want to form beneficial new beliefs, it is more a process of unlearning and replacing old beliefs, and you will meet with resistance as these old patterns fight back. This is how you know when you are close to your belief boundaries, you feel _comfortable_ within the boundaries of your belief system and you feel uncomfortable and fearful beyond the boundary.

Nevertheless, when you are awakened to your own power within you do have the choice of what you want to believe and to selectively believe in things that are beneficial, while eliminating sabotaging beliefs.

You will expose yourself to ideas, thoughts, and people that support your beneficial beliefs and avoid the opposite, thereby creating your reality in a larger framework. You enlarge the boundaries of what you are capable of by getting over fear and getting out of your comfort zone, and eventually expand your comfort zone and your abilities.

Unfortunately, many people run their lives like a hard-written script, never growing conscious enough to examine and consciously change their sabotaging beliefs into beneficial ones. They do not know that they can expand their boundaries, instead settling with restriction. To some people, they simply fear the unknown and prefer their own comfort zone.

Many people are subject to a type of mass "brainwash", instead of consciously choosing what they are exposed to and what they want to believe in. They live life as a victim. They let go of their greatest power, the power of choice.

Perhaps you feel that you didn't have a choice of family or cultural background to be born into, or the set of beliefs you were infused with at an early age. But there might come a moment when you realize that you have ***total control*** of what you want to believe.

The process of "unlearning" harmful thinking patterns and disadvantageous beliefs from an early age is very crucial because, when you realize that you can choose what you believe in, you can begin "reprogramming" your mind for powerful conscious creation.

The power is in realizing that you always do have the choice and then venture out of your comfort zone.

Belief is the boundary within which you create your personal realities. Examine your beliefs and expand those that are limiting you and what you can achieve. Don't think blindly, instead think about how you think.

When you examine how you think you are getting onto higher grounds and probing your beliefs. Ask yourself constantly, "is it true?"

How do you know it's true for you?

Is there an expanded and more beneficial view to what you have in mind?

When you bring how you think into your conscious thinking you will then be able to expand the boundary, within which you can navigate with more freedom. Know that what you can achieve is boundless.

Peace and Harmony: What You Truly Want

Sometimes it is obvious that something, or someone, is "brainwashing" us. We are conditioned to think in a certain way, almost as if we are funneled into a container.

The other day my husband was exposed to an ad on the internet (don't you like how many ads we are "forced" to watch every day?). The ad went into detail, describing a series of symptoms, and then coined a new, yet odd, term to define a "new" disease. Next, the ad introduced its magical solution: the drug it was advertising.

We are excellent at raising awareness of diseases and mishaps. People go to great lengths to define fancy new diseases, exposing us to ideas and beliefs in ill health.

We are bombarded with negative news, terrorist stories, natural disasters, depressing events, corruption, scandals, whatever attracts the attention from the conscious mind, generating fear, anxiety, and stress. Negative emotions are a strong force for consumption, with profits to be made from them.

Many things we are exposed to under the disguise of "goodwill" are actually harming us. Let's take health as an example again. There are countless anti-this disease, anti-that disease groups out there. Our psychological obligations make us feel that it is righteous to support such groups and to join up. If you are not anti-cancer, after all, then you must be pro-cancer!

However, the subconscious mind does not understand negatives. When you say "anti-cancer", you are actually tuning into the energies of cancer, the very thing that you are against. This applies to all negatives.

The reason is this: if I say, "don't think of a green pig", the very thing you think of is a green pig. For the mind to understand what is not, it must tune in to what it is. The subconscious mind ignores the negatives; you can make it negative on the conscious level but deep down you are tuning into the energy of the very thing you are against.

When you focus attention on anti-cancer, you might feel fear, anger, or grief over a lost loved one, or some other negative emotion. You are feeding into the energy of cancer, even though that's the last thing you want to do on the conscious level. In essence, by putting your attention there, you are giving it power and promoting the very thing you are against.

With such harmful consequences, then, why are so many people obsessed with anti-disease, anti-war, or anti-something unpleasant?

First off, the vast majority of innocent people who get involved in such activities do not understand the reality in their minds; they aren't aware of how the mind works, entering the cause with pure intent to do the right thing. They do not understand that they are tuning into the same negative feelings and emotions that could lead to the things that they are against, feeding the negative power unconsciously.

Secondly, and potentially a powerful driving force, is the small group of people with ill intent. They know that they are promoting negativity but do so for their own financial gain.

People consume when they are in FEAR. By putting the masses in the fear of cancer, a lot of profit can be gained. Therefore, raising awareness of cancer and starting causes against it to further funnel people into this "container" makes it easier to "manipulate" the mass.

I don't mean that you should never join any groups that raise awareness of illness, natural disaster, mass killing, war, or anything unpleasant or fearful, because it is your freedom of choice. What I suggest is that you become more conscious and see things from a higher perspective, with the understanding of the power of your own mind. Whatever you put your attention to, you give it power.

Where would you like to direct your attention to?

Is it disease or health?

Is it poverty or wealth?

Is it war or peace?

It is human nature to want health and peace but "anti-disease" or "anti-war" is not the best way to obtain it. There are many ways to stray from harmony and you don't need to pick out one non-harmonic state as your target of hatred, such as cancer. Don't give negative things your power.

Why not raise awareness of peace and harmony? How about we focus all of our attention on peace and harmony? I know that's what you truly want...

Mind Reality is The Only Reality There is - And You Are an Expression of Higher Consciousness

Understand the true power of your mind and start living expansively. Cultivate your mind continuously and make choices from a higher perspective. Get in touch with your mind because reality is in your own mind, where you have full control.

Your body is in a particular state at a particular moment according to your state of mind at that moment; it has nothing to do with physical reality.

You think of a happy memory from the past and it makes you feel so pleasant that you could not help but smile. To someone observing you, it is odd because there is nothing in the physical world that could have made you do that.

You react to your mental states, and your body is a perfect reflection of your mental state. Even if you are living in the moment and smile because of what you see now in the physical reality, it is still your mind that perceived the physical reality and translated it into a pleasant sensation, and then reacted to that sensation. In fact, it is your own conscious mind that created the feeling of physical reality out of energies. You are never out of the framework of your mind. Mind reality is all there is, it's the only reality. And you have full control of this reality.

Every individual has different perceptions through their respective minds, to the extent that they may not even be comparable.

Imagine that you have a shared experience with a friend. You both had the same teacher who was so strict in elementary school. Twenty years later, you get together and discuss school experiences. Of course, each of you can only access your own mind, limited by your own views and beliefs. While you two chat away you realize that you perceived the same teacher and related events so differently, to the extent that you could not agree at all with your friend's description of what happened. Perhaps you benefited from the teacher being strict while your friend hated what the teacher did.

You see, you each create your own mental impressions of people and events. These perceptions are influenced by so many mental factors that you each look at them through different filters.

Which interpretation is real?

They are both imaginations. If one hundred people witnessed the same people and event, you would get a lot more versions of the same story, each filtered through their own minds. It is impossible to say which one is right because, when the mind perceives, it is subjective.

I agree with Ruth Hubbard who said, "Truth is in the eye of the beholder". In fact, I would say truth is in the mind of the beholder.

Whatever is perceived is heavily influenced by beliefs and ideas, but each will be "true" to the person perceiving it; it's just that their realities are different.

Sure, some things like beautiful flowers are perceived as beautiful by multiple minds, and we can believe we share the same perceptions.

We share the physical reality because we **participate** in it; this makes us believe that reality is absolute and that we are perceiving the same reality, which of course is not true.

There are always subtle differences in our perceptions. Each of us creates our own reality in our own minds and no two minds are the same. We each live in our different "reality" or, rather, in our own illusions of the mind.

Since we are the ones creating our own mind projections, we also control what we create. We can create better illusions that serve us and abandon those that sabotage us; but it has nothing to do with "physical reality" because there is none.

Perception is only possible through the mind; the perception of physical reality is a mind creation. There is no absolute reality unless you remove the mind, in which case there won't be any perception at all, therefore, no sense of reality at all. In essence, the only thing relevant to an individual is his/her personal reality in the mind. Reality is in the mind of the beholder.

But what is the mind?

What is the consciousness that you know as "you"?

How are your mind and body related?

What are YOU exactly?

You are an expression of higher consciousness, perceiving outwards through your physical senses and inwards through your intuition. Your body is a vehicle through which the true "you" perceives and understands itself. Your body is the temple where you reside. You are an expression of consciousness.

In addition, whatever form you see, hear, touch, or anything you perceive, is also an expression of consciousness taking on different forms.

To understand that forms are expressions of consciousness, let's take the example of painting. Painters train their visual acuity as well as their imagination; they observe the fine details that people don't usually pay attention to. Then they must express their understanding through a paint brush on a canvas. The idea in their mind is laid out elegantly. As a result, a beautiful painting is created.

It might seem that the painting came out of nothingness, but thought is behind it; the painting is a pure expression of thought, of consciousness. Consciousness takes on form; form is created out of consciousness.

The same applies to music or other types of art, objects, flowers, trees, a blade of grass, houses, furniture, or anything you perceive. There's a thought, an idea behind every form, and that includes your flesh. There's an intelligence behind it, expressing itself as the form that you perceive.

Two things at play here: the life essence and the form - the invisible and the visible. The two are so intertwined and our physical senses can only understand the obvious one on the physical level. However, you are not the form that you take on.

When two cars are racing each other, one driver might say: "I'm faster than you". What he really saying is: "My car is faster than your car". In this case, the driver identifies with his car and the car becomes an extension of him.

Similarly, our body is our vehicle, we are so good at driving this vehicle that we mentally merged with this vehicle. We identify with our physical body in a very subtle way.

If our body is our vehicle, when did we enter this vehicle?

Now, think back to a time when you were a baby. Chances are you do not remember when you were inside the body of a baby. However, you can observe newborns and babies.

A baby cannot use her eyes effectively. Her two eyes cannot coordinate well enough when trying to look at things. She has no idea what her arms and hands can do, perhaps she eventually manages to swing an arm and landed her finger in her mouth. She started to suckle the finger. She got the sensation of suckling her fingers and she learned how it feels. When she stops suckling, the sensation on the thumb caused by the suckling stops. She made a conclusion about her behavior and what it can bring.

She continues to learn new things about her body. She learns that she has control over her bodily parts, and how it feels to move each bodily part. She's learning about her body exponentially, just like a new driver learns how to drive a car.

When this baby reaches a year old, she realized that she can put her hands on a table, chair, couch or anything that can support her. If she bends her knees in a certain way and pushes on those legs, she can actually get up straight. Of course, her legs start to wobble, and she falls back into the sitting position. She continues to try and eventually she got it! She's standing tall. Now her view totally changes. She just reached a whole new level of integrating with the body of a baby!

Does the process we learn how to use our body feel like learning to drive a car? Our body is just our vehicle and we entered this vehicle so early in life, that we don't even have conscious memory of entering this vehicle. Therefore, we never questioned it and never really dug deep into the question of who we really are beyond the flesh and bone.

We entered this vehicle called our body BEFORE we developed the ability to remember things CONSCIOUSLY. No wonder using our body to walk, talk, eat feels so natural to us, and we even confuse our body as the real "I".

However, the ears are not the one that hears; the eyes are not the ones that sees; the skin is not the one that feels the touch; the tough is not the one that tastes. The MIND is.

The mind is the one that's perceiving though different "channels" of the body. Your consciousness is the TRUE observer. You are the one behind the driver seat.

You are a powerful life force, an eternal energy being, a soul entity. You have much more power than you give yourself credit for.

You are a being, a consciousness; you are pure energy, a life force. You can't be named. Any name is only temporary and does not tell what you are.

You can't be defined. To define is to confine.

You can't be destroyed, and you never die.

You are in the process of shedding forms and taking on new forms and, in this process, you become more and more aware of your true being.

You express yourself outwards and the form (your body) is what you see. You are an expression of higher consciousness. You chose this body in this lifetime to fulfil a grand mission.

You, the consciousness, are a state of being. You are in the process of becoming what you really are and doing what you are capable of. You are heading towards fully expressing what you are, and life is the process of the unfoldment into your true being.

You are a perfect expression. To uncover your greatest power for healing, personal empowerment, and fulfillment in life, you need to get in touch with the real YOU. You have all the answers that you are seeking and create realities in your mind to reach your destination.

But your journey is more important than the destination, because you are constantly in a state of being, you are in the process of becoming more and more of who you are.

The so called "destination" is a state of being that you desire, but it's just a state of being like others in a constant flow of change. The journey to get to your perceived "destination" is a process of changing your state of being as well, and that's what matters most to you.

There is no "destination" and the journey is not the means to get to the perceived destination. The journey is all there is and the state of being is all there is. Enjoy every step along the journey. Enjoy your state of being. Enjoy every breath.

You are brave enough to have entered a physical body, knowing that you will temporarily forget your true home of eternal love. You entered this life to challenge yourself and gain the greatest learning experience possible.

What if you could open up your awareness to your soul mind, aligning it with your conscious mind?

What if you could live from a higher perspective as your true self?

What if you become an embodiment of the energy of LOVE?

What if you tap into the power of your mind for better relationships?

What if you unleash your power for business success?

What would life feel like then?

Would you be able to follow your life's purpose and live to your fullest potential and benefit humanity?

What if you could get help from your true self and other advanced soul beings?

Your ability is UNLIMITED.

Your conscious mind is the window through which you focus your attention. But, as you have seen, you have the choice of living from a larger sense, where you see no boundaries. It's your choice.

You do not have to confine your awareness anymore.

Cultivate your mind continuously and persistently, for you will create a peaceful and harmonious reality by getting in touch with the real YOU.

You are not a physical being with a soul, you are a soul being with a physical body.

Your imagination is your greatest power.

When you use your imagination purposefully you are expressing your power as an energy soul being. You are shifting and molding physical realities. Imagination is how YOU, as a soul, manifest realities.

Everything is imagination. It is your greatest tool as a powerful creator. Imagine, and it is.

This is The Nature of Mind Realities.